Active LEARNING

Increasing Flow in the Classroom

Pat Hollingsworth and Gina Lewis

Crown House Publishing Ltd.
www.crownhouse.co.uk

First published by:
Crown House Publishing Ltd.
Crown Buildings, Bancyfelin, Carmarthen, Wales SA33 5ND, UK
www.crownhouse.co.uk

and

Crown House Publishing Company LLC
4 Berkeley Street, Norwalk, CT 06850, USA
www.CHPUS.com

Editing: Melanie Mallon
Design, typesetting, and cover: Sheryl Shetler
Photos: All photos by the authors, taken at University School, University of Tulsa, Oklahoma.
Illustrations: All illustrations by Pat Hollingsworth unless otherwise indicated.

Printed in the United States of America
ISBN-13: 978–1–904424–59–8
ISBN-10: 1–904424–59–7

Library of Congress Cataloging-in-Publication Data

Hollingsworth, Patricia.
    Active learning : increasing flow in the classroom / Pat Hollingsworth and Gina Lewis.
        p. cm.
    Includes bibliographical references (p.   ) and index.
    ISBN-13: 978-1-904424-59-8 (alk. paper)
    ISBN-10: 1-904424-59-7 (alk. paper)
    1. Active learning.   I. Lewis, Gina. II. Title.
    LB1027.23.H66 2006
    372.139--dc22

                                                                                            2005024232

Contents

Introduction

Rationale for Active Learning

This book was written by practicing teachers who are driven to provide the best, most meaningful learning experiences for each and every one of their students. This unifying purpose provides the intellectual vigor that creates a learning atmosphere where students are highly engaged and involved.

In this book, these experienced classroom teachers share their most useful and engrossing ways to create optimal learning experiences for all students, practical strategies that have been used with students of all ages, from preschool through graduate school. These teachers know that getting and keeping students' attention is vital to the learning process.

In *Flow* (1990), Mihaly Csikszentmihalyi describes attention as a type of mental and emotional energy. Flow is a state of consciousness in which a person becomes so totally immersed in an activity that time flies by unnoticed. He says that true "enjoyment happens only as a result of unusual investments of attention" (46). In other words, pleasure can be felt without effort (by electrical or chemical methods on pleasure points in the brain), but full enjoyment cannot.

Csikszentmihalyi (1997) says that to experience flow you have to expend additional mental and emotional energy. A life filled with exciting flow experiences is more worth living than one spent consuming passive entertainment. Neurologist Richard Restak confirms the wisdom of active experiences: "The 'use it or lose it' formula applies to each of us no matter what our age. Moreover, the exercise of our brain's inherent powers is highly pleasurable" (2001, 14). This is a lesson for us as well as for students. In this book, teachers vividly describe ways to use and direct mental and emotional energy with the goal of creating lasting and more meaningful learning that leads to flow experiences. The long-term benefits for students who understand and experience flow include a greater chance of them discovering a passion that might guide them toward particular careers or deeply satisfying hobbies. There is also a greater likelihood that they will embrace lifelong learning and be more willing to take chances, persist through initial challenges, and overcome fear and apprehension in school, work, and their personal lives simply by harnessing the power of flow.

The opportunity for the flow experience to occur is greatly enhanced when individuals are having what Dan Rea (2003) calls "serious-fun." Educators encourage serious-fun by having high expectations for work quality and by orchestrating engaging classroom activities. Active learning that emphasizes "serious-fun" can help students focus their attention, increase their enjoyment of learning, and set the stage for flow experiences.

The lesson steps in this book are similar to those that create flow: Students understand and relate to goals, become immersed in the activity, pay attention to what is happening, and learn to enjoy the immediate experience. Lessons describe ways to combine goal setting, active learning, and self-reflection to help students reach optimal experiences.

Pat's Introduction to Active Learning

I was introduced to active learning early in my life. My grandmother delighted in the visual world and in storytelling. She taught me to love the birds, trees, and flowers of our rural North Carolina community. She told me wonderful stories that fired my imagination. Her teaching method was active. We walked in the yard looking at plants and flowers. We put out food for the birds, which she identified as they came to the feeder. I picked up acorns and fed them to the pigs. I helped plant, weed, and harvest in the garden. My grandmother encouraged me to be an active learner and to reflect on what I had learned by drawing pictures about it.

As a teacher, I have always been able to understand how students feel when they have to sit and listen for long periods without a break. In similar situations, my eyes glaze over and my mind wanders just as theirs do. Over the years I have learned what good teachers everywhere have learned: Meaningful and lasting learning must engage the learner. "The brain is biologically programmed to attend first to information that has strong emotional content" (Wolfe 2001, 88). We have to get and keep student attention. We have to tap into their emotions.

I recently read that every cell in our bodies has an emotional component (Shanor 1999). We have feelings about everything we do. When those feelings are positive, we are more likely to pay attention and be engaged. My positive experiences with learning, and probably yours also, brought me to and have kept me teaching.

"We know emotion is very important to the educative process because it drives attention, which drives learning and memory" (Sylwester 1995, 106). Most of us go into fields of study because of the positive experiences and emotions that we associate with the field. These are the kinds of experiences that we as teachers want to encourage in students.

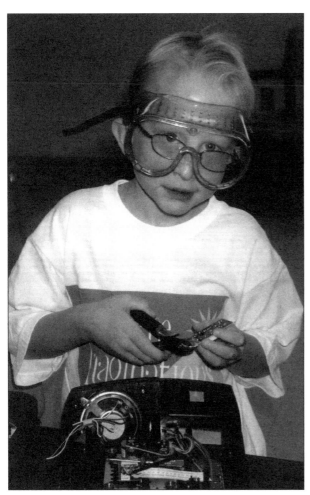

CREATIVE INVENTOR

What Is Active Learning?

Students are actively learning when they are intensely engaged, mentally or physically. Active learning is vigorous, lively, energetic, intense, strong, and effective. Active learning is involved learning; it takes place when the learners are excited, mentally alert, and caught up in the experience. The lessons in this book include many strategies to keep learners alert and engaged. Here are a few examples of ways that active learning can increase flow in the classroom.

Relating to Goals

When teachers are explicit about the goals of learning, students understand and relate to what they are to gain from various lessons. This is an essential first step when introducing a lesson. Students need to feel a part of this process. To facilitate this, each lesson plan includes a section called Measurable Learning Objectives, which summarizes lesson aims to share with students, and a section near the end called Reflection, which includes advice on helping students reflect on the experience to determine how well they reached their goals and whether they experienced elements of flow during the lesson.

Engaging Students

Teachers often instinctively know that to make learning more meaningful, students must exert more mental and emotional energy. In other words, we often want students to reach the state of flow—but just wanting this to happen does not make it happen. The thoughtfully planned, engaging activities in this book keep students mentally alert and absorbed.

Using Art, Movement, and the Senses

The lesson strategies are designed to employ as many of the five senses as possible to fully engage students. The arts are an ideal way to employ a variety of the senses, encourage students' sense of community, provide multiple tools for discovering and expressing meaning, build confidence in and enthusiasm about learning, and reinforce the cornerstones of all learning: our cognitive, emotional, attentional, and motor systems (Sylwester 2004; Jensen 2001). Rules for Art and Life (pages 68 and 76), Exploring the World of Artists (page 83), and Active Learning to Develop Goals (page 9) encourage sensory learning, particularly through sight, touch, hearing, and smell.

Many of the lessons also use the strategy of physical movement to engage students. Movement Arts (page 25), History of Architecture (page 93), Thor and the Missing Hammer (page 31), and The Story of the Trojan Horse (page 41) use bodily movement extensively.

Varying the Pace and Activities

To keep minds alert and active, vary the pace and type of activities. Each of the lessons provides ideas for changing the pace, and each lesson is readily adaptable so that you can easily add your own ideas for variety. Active learning can be mental as well as physical. Changing from large group work to individual work to small group work is just one easy and effective way to vary the mental pace.

THE JOY OF THE ARTS!

How to Incorporate Active Learning into Your Classroom

Identify for your students when you are incorporating active learning lessons. Students will anticipate them with pleasure. Use the lessons in any way you choose; the following methods will help you devote time for them.

DAILY TIME: ACTIVE LEARNING TO FIT YOUR STUDENTS

(Daily: 15 to 30 minutes)

- All students need opportunities for movement in the classroom. By providing them a few minutes each day to do lessons like Movement Arts (page 25), you will help your students be ready and alert for learning.

- All students need to know about the flow experience and how it can enhance their lives, as explored in Active Learning in the Classroom (page 3).

- Students need the opportunity to think about what success would mean for them and how they will go about achieving it (see Active Learning to Develop Goals, page 9).

- Students need time to learn to draw. In addition to the person and clown drawings (see pages 68 and 76), you can use this same technique to teach a variety of subjects, such as parts of an insect, parts of a fish, parts of flowers, the planets, states, continents, countries, and so forth.

- Some students need help learning to monitor their behaviors. You will save time by helping those students use a daily behavior chart (see Active Learning to Improve Behavior, on page 16).

WEEKLY SPECIAL EVENTS TIME: ACTIVE LEARNING LESSONS THAT FIT YOUR CURRICULUM

(Weekly: 30 minutes to 1 hour)

Have a weekly active learning time, or use these lessons more regularly in your classroom.

- All schools curricula include reading, math, and social studies. Choose the lessons that fit with what you already teach.

- The drama lessons range from kindergarten through middle school. Every social studies subject that you teach can be enhanced by adding a drama component. This can be a skit done in class to review facts or a fully realized and rehearsed play for an audience.

- Animal Studies in 18 Steps (page 182) can be adapted to include all academic subjects.

- The lesson on *Charlotte's Web* (page 146) can be adapted to any book that your class is reading.

- Word Works (page 140), which teaches both reading and writing, is a great way to get students excited about those subjects.

- The lessons on writing and parts of speech (Take the Fear Out, page 156, and Become the Adverb, page 136) are active and involving for students.

- The math lessons are fun and fit well into the regular school curriculum (see Student-Created Math Games, page 166, and Guess-and-Check Tables, page 171).

- The History of Architecture (page 93) would work well as a weekly event.

MONTHLY SPECIAL EVENTS TIME: ACTIVE LEARNING IN THE ARTS
(Monthly: 1 to 2 hours)

During a monthly special event time, introduce one of the art lessons, such as Copland's Rodeo (page 60) or Exploring the World of Artists (page 83), or try Movement Arts (page 25), a play (such as Thor and the Missing Hammer, page 31, The Story of the Trojan Horse, page 41, or Make Social Studies Come Alive, page 53), or a drawing lesson (see the two Rules for Art and Life lessons, on pages 68 and 76). This might be a time to invite parents to visit.

Providing High Expectations

You will be most successful in helping students reach flow when you have high expectations of work quality, help students relate to and set goals, use engaging art-related strategies, and vary the pace—in other words, when you encourage serious-fun. The expectation of high quality work is crucial for the flow experience to occur.

Using This Book

- **Lesson plan format.** The active learning lesson plans are intended to guide you, not restrict the way you approach or use the material. Be creative and encourage your students to be involved in the ways that work best for them.

- **Sections in italics.** Throughout the lessons, passages in italics are first-person teacher narratives, scripts to give you an idea of what you might say directly to students. Of course, you will say things the way you want to say them. The italicized text is only a suggestion. If you decide that you do not need examples of what to say to students, just skip these sections and focus on the non-italicized lesson steps.

Part 1: Creating an Atmosphere for Flow

Chapters 1–3 provide active learning strategies that relate to appropriate class-room behavior. Students need a safe, caring environment in order to think, learn, and be ready for flow experiences. These chapters provide some ideas to support that need.

Part 2: Active Learning in the Arts

Chapter 4–13 focus on active learning in the arts. Each chapter is written so that any teacher, regardless of educational background or experience in the arts, can implement the lesson in the classroom. Many school systems have cut back on the arts. These lessons will make it possible for you to introduce music, drama, drawing, and the history of art and architecture to your class while reinforcing the existing curriculum.

Part 3: Active Learning Everywhere

Chapters 14–21 cover a range of academic subjects from language arts and math to research and science. Every subject can become an active learning lesson. Once you begin using active learning strategies in your lessons, you will likely begin adding them to all you do with students. Active learning is addictive, and it will lead to flow for you and your students.

Part One

Creating an Atmosphere for Flow

Chapter 1

Active Learning in the Classroom

Helping Students Recognize Flow

— Pat Hollingsworth —

Grades: 3–8

Time Frame Options

- Introduction: two 30-minute sessions
- Independent practice: 15 to 20 minutes per day

Measurable Learning Objectives

Share these aims with students:

- Students will learn to identify flow experiences in their lives.
- Students will identify the elements of the flow experience.

Active Learning in the Classroom

A major goal of this book is to provide engaging classroom activities to help lead students to the flow experience. Therefore, one of the first active learning activities to do with students is to discuss *Flow,* both the book and the experience.

Materials

- ☐ white paper (several sheets per student)
- ☐ pencils, pens, and colored markers for each student
- ☐ spiral notebook for each student

Supplementary Materials

- ☐ large sheet of poster paper or photocopier that enlarges to poster size or 11" x 17"
- ☐ copy of *Flow* (Csikszentmihalyi 1990)

Preparation

1. Create a class flow chart, either by enlarging the example on page 5 or by using it as a model to draw a chart on poster paper.

2. Post the flow chart in an area where students can easily write on it, such as low on a bulletin board or wall.

3. Distribute paper, notebooks, pencils, pens, and markers to students.

 ## Getting Students Excited about the Topic

Begin by asking students if they have ever been so wrapped up in an activity that they lost track of time. For example:

> **❝**Have you ever had a time when you have been so involved with what you were doing that you lost track of what time it was or even where you were? Some people have this experience when drawing, or putting together a puzzle, or creating a sand castle. When has this happened to you?**❞**

Class Flow Chart

Student's Name	Date	Type of Activity	Feelings about the Experience

Guided Practice

1. Define *flow* experiences and the source of the idea. Discuss Csikszentmihalyi's ideas about flow, energy, and attention and encourage students to contribute their own ideas to the discussion, particularly what they think about the idea of people creating their identities when they choose where to focus their attention. For example:

   > **"** *Dr. Mihalyi Csikszentmihalyi* [ME-high CHICK-sent-me-high-ee] *has written a book about these experiences that he calls 'flow.' He says that people choose how they will focus their attention. He says that we create ourselves by how we use our energy. What do you think he means?* **"**

2. Next, share some of your own flow experiences and have students again think of times when they have had these experiences. Have them close their eyes and visualize these times, reliving the experiences.

   > **"** *Thank you for sharing your ideas. I often have a flow experience when I am doing artwork, sometimes when I am writing, and often when I am reading. I want you to think about times when you lost track of time and space. Now close your eyes and imagine one or more of those times. You were fully focused. All your energy was concentrated on that one experience. You were feeling joyful and serene. Maybe you were decorating a bulletin board or your room at home, or perhaps you were drawing or coloring, playing a board game, building a model, or playing an instrument.* **"**

3. Then share the aims of the lesson, as described in the Measurable Learning Objectives section, so that students can understand and relate to the learning goals.

Independent Practice

1. Have students draw and write about the experiences they visualized, using a new sheet of paper for each experience. Give them plenty of time to think about the experiences before they describe—in pictures, words, or both—what they were doing and what it was like.

THE FLOW OF MUSIC

2. Next, invite students to share their experiences with the class:

> 66 *I want you to share your flow experiences with the class. Be sure that you listen respectfully to each person. We want everyone to feel this is a safe environment in which to describe these experiences. Everyone who wishes to will have a turn. Who would like to start?* 99

3. After everyone has had a chance to share, explain to students that they will be keeping track of times when they experience flow by writing about the experiences in the spiral notebooks—their flow journals. You might explain it like this:

> 66 *Now make an entry in your spiral notebook. This will be your flow journal, your record of all the flow experiences you have during the school year. Each time you think of a flow experience, make an entry. Be sure to include the date, and feel free to draw as well as write about your flow experiences. We will have time each morning for you to make entries in your flow journals.* 99

Closure

Close the lesson by describing the class flow chart as a place to share flow experiences:

> **"**On the back wall is a class flow chart, where you can record each time you do something that leads you to have a flow experience. Flow is a joyous experience that we want to have in our lives, and it is helpful to be able to identify what it is and how it comes about. Our chart will help us pay attention to these positive experiences.**"**

Evaluation

- Students will be able to identify and share experiences of flow.

- Students will add flow experiences to the class flow chart as the school year progresses.

Reflection

Ask students to share examples of how they reached the goals of this lesson. This could be an oral discussion or a writing assignment.

Extension

- Students could create experiments to determine whether flow experiences can be enhanced by certain environmental changes, such as particular music or other background sounds, certain lighting, a specific room temperature, and so forth.

- Students could receive extra credit for reading *Flow* and writing a report or giving a presentation on the book to the class.

Chapter 2

Active Learning
to Develop Goals

A Visual Symbol of Success

— Liz Jarnigan —

Grades: 3–8

Time Frame Options

- Introduction: two 30-minute sessions
- Independent practice: three or four 30-minute sessions

Measurable Learning Objectives

Share this aim with students:

Students will demonstrate how to represent ideas in both verbal and visual contexts by creating their own symbols for success.

Active Learning to Develop Goals

Coaches often use visual aids, such as films, photographs, and drawings, to help athletes improve their basic skills and overall performances. Visual examples can help people better understand their performance responsibilities and can keep them mentally alert and active.

Stephen Covey (1989), internationally known speaker and author, writes about how he uses visualization to help people keep their values before them. He says that "almost all of the world-class athletes and other peak performers are visualizers" (134). Legendary UCLA basketball coach John Wooden's Pyramid of Success is a visual model he created over the course of his lengthy career as a basketball player and coach; he records within a pyramid the keywords he associates with success. He suggests that the technique is meaningful both in the game of basketball and in life (Wooden 2003). By organizing his philosophy of success visually, his ideas become more memorable and more accessible to everyone.

Materials

- ☐ Wooden's *Inch and Miles* (2003)
- ☐ one copy of the Visual Symbols of Success examples on page 13
- ☐ paper (a few sheets for each student) and pencils
- ☐ miscellaneous arts and crafts supplies, such as scissors, construction paper, markers, and glue
- ☐ student flow journals (see page 7)

Supplementary Materials

- ☐ Overhead projector with transparencies and markers
- ☐ Other books by John Wooden, such as *Wooden: A Lifetime of Observations and Reflections On and Off the Court* (Wooden and Jamison 1997). See also www.coachwooden.com.
- ☐ Stephen Covey's *Seven Habits of Highly Effective People* (1989).

Preparation

1. Read *Inch and Miles* (or at least the building blocks of success, on page 38 of Wooden's book).

2. Create your own visual symbol before introducing the concept to students: Brainstorm a list of success words and put them into a visual symbol, such as an apple or a schoolhouse. Fill the image with success words.

 Getting Students Excited about the Topic

1. Introduce the topic of success, discussing with students what success means. For example:

   66 *Have you ever wondered what it would be like to be famous and successful? Does being successful mean having a lot of money? Or does it mean something else? Today we are going to brainstorm what you think success means.* 99

SETTING GOALS WITH FRIENDS

2. Discuss with students how people use visualization to help them achieve their goals. You might use an example from Stephen Covey's book or show Wooden's pyramid to the class. For example:

   66 *Many people realize the value of being able to visualize their goals. Stephen Covey does this in his book* The Seven Habits of Highly Effective People. *He has graphics and charts that show his goals, such as an upward spiral with the words 'learn,' 'do,' and 'commit.' Even without seeing that graphic, you are able to get a mental image of what is important to him.* 99

3. Tell students that you will be reading from *Inch and Miles* to help them think about what success is and how to visualize various aspects of success. Explain that Wooden's book shows how to define success in verbal and visual ways, and that this will help students create their own visual symbols of success. Share the aims of the lesson, as described in the Measurable Learning Objectives section, so that students can understand and relate to the learning goal.

Guided Practice

1. Read Wooden's building blocks of success (2003, 38) one at a time to the students. After reading each building block, ask the students,

   ❝*What does that mean to you? What other words might you use? What other ways might you visualize this idea?***❞**

2. List Wooden's and students' words on the board as you go. Do this for each of Wooden's 15 building blocks. These discussions and the list on the board will help students fully understand their task.

3. Use an overhead or chalkboard to demonstrate how to create a visual symbol of success by re-creating the symbol you made earlier. Show the examples of symbols on pages 13 (the karate belt, star, and arrow).

4. Discuss the meaning of the word "symbol." Ask students why they think Wooden used a pyramid for his symbol.

5. Have students brainstorm a list of symbols. Write or draw the ideas on the board.

6. Write down your success words, then put them into the visual symbol you chose (such as an apple or schoolhouse). Tell students why you chose the symbol you did and explain your words.

7. Emphasize that each student should create his or her own symbol, different from yours and from each other's—it should represent what is important to the student as an individual. Show students the examples on page 13 and describe them.

Visual Symbols of Success

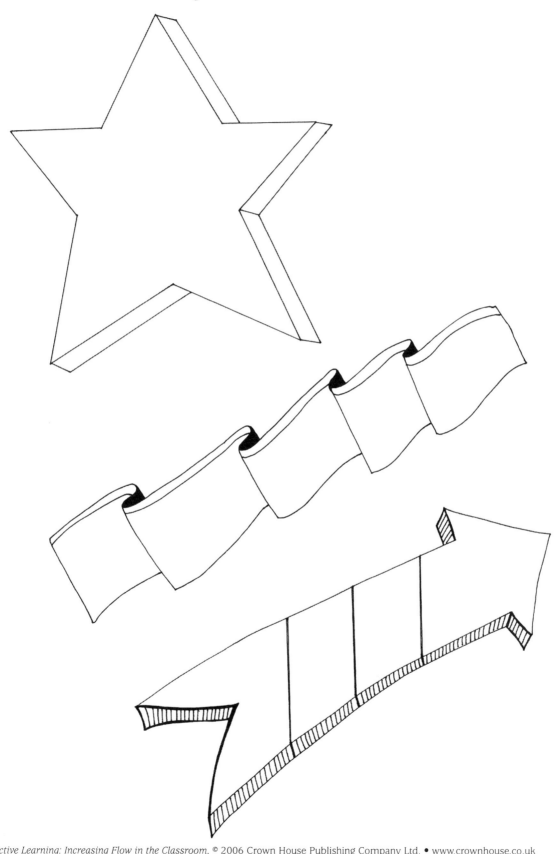

Independent Practice

1. Explain to students that they will now create visual symbols of what success means to them. Review the steps of the project before the students begin:

   ▪ *First, select words that describe what success in life means to you.*

   ▪ *Put those words into a visual symbol or picture that best expresses your ideas. The visual symbol should be uniquely meaningful to your personal ideas of success.*

   ▪ *To finish, write an explanation of your personal ideas of success by describing how each word fits into the symbol or picture you have created. For example, one person used a star to symbolize being a light in the world. She said that the five people in her family help her reach this goal. The words in the middle described the heart of her family, which is loving and caring. When her family is remembering their religious faith and showing loving kindness, they are being successful and helping the world.*

   ▪ *Be prepared to share your visual symbol of success with the class.*

2. Distribute various arts and crafts materials for students to use in creating their symbols for success. Provide feedback as the students are working. Let them know that you value their unique approaches to creating a visual symbol.

Closure

Congratulate the class on their thoughtful work on what success means to each of them, then have students take turns presenting and explaining their symbols.

Evaluation

Evaluate student symbols using criteria such as creative use of ideas; original symbol choice; well thought-out relationship between words and image; and well-written description of the symbol's meaning.

Reflection

▪ Ask students to share examples of how they reached the goals of this lesson. This could be an oral discussion or a writing assignment.

ARTIST AT WORK

- Discuss with your students any aspects of flow that they experienced and add the information to the class flow chart (see page 5). Then ask students to make entries in their flow journals (see page 7).

Extension

- Have the students share with the class examples of other visual symbols they encounter either during the school day or away from school, such as a stop sign, a food pyramid, or a bull's-eye. Ask them if the image helps them remember the information in the symbol.

- Use this exercise at the beginning of a school year and repeat it throughout (students may wish to revise their symbols as the year progresses). Show students' visual symbols to parents at conference times throughout the school year.

- Have the students apply their visual symbols for success toward at least one goal in each of their classes for the school year.

Chapter 3

Active Learning to Improve Behavior

It's All about Control

— Pat Hollingsworth —

Active Learning to Improve Behavior

Not completing assigned work, disrupting the learning experience for others, and generally being off task are common types of inappropriate classroom behavior. Class disruptions are overt ways of being in control, and off-task and noncompliant behaviors are passive ways of being in control. Helping individual students actively monitor their behavior is a way to give them authentic control over their lives.

As long as students are unwilling to give of themselves to school activities, they keep themselves out of the state of flow and thus out of the joy that many academic activities can bring. This chapter describes how to develop monitoring systems that, with the help of a student's parents, will help that student improve his or her behavior.

Grades: PreK–6

Time Frame Options

- Preparation: 20 minutes
- Subsequent days: 10 minutes daily (for three months to one year)

Measurable Learning Objectives

Share this aim with students:

Individual students will improve their behavior by being in charge of their own monitoring.

Materials

- ☐ Teacher's Record of Student Progress (page 21)
- ☐ Student Behavior Chart (page 22), one copy for each day of the week
- ☐ student flow journal (see page 7)

Preparation

1. When a student has more than one teacher, every teacher will have to use the system to make it effective. Discuss it with them before getting the parents' cooperation.

2. Discuss the problem behavior with the student's parents and explain the monitoring system you would like to try.

3. Show parents the Student Behavior Chart (page 22) and explain that for every appropriate behavior, the student receives 10 minutes of preferred activity time, and for every inappropriate behavior, 10 minutes are subtracted from the preferred activity time.

4. Explain that you need their help in following through with the appropriate amount of reward time for their child. Ask them to sign the chart each day for the student to return the next day.

5. Let parents know that you will be using the same system in class during the school day. Tell them that the method will be much more effective if you are all working together on the problem.

Getting Students Excited about the Topic

Show the student the chart as you talk together privately, sharing the aim of the chart (see Measurable Learning Objectives) and emphasizing that the student might enjoy the process. For example, you might say,

" You have been having some problems in class that are troublesome for you, your classmates, your parents, and for me as your teacher. I want us to try a new system that I think you will like. I have talked with your parents, and they hope it will help you. You will have a chart on a clipboard that you will have on your desk and also take with you everywhere you go at school, such as specialty classes, recess, and lunch. "

Guided Practice

1. Point out that the student should fill in the name and date on the chart that you will give him or her each day.

2. Note the times listed on the lefthand side and explain that for every 15 minutes of the day, the student will chart his or her behavior in either the Appropriate Behavior column or the Inappropriate Behavior column. Tell the student that you will also keep a chart of the student's behavior.

3. Explain that appropriate behavior leads to 10 minutes of reward time and inappropriate behavior leads to 10 minutes' less reward time. For example:

" If you have eight positive comments in one day, that adds up to 80 minutes of preferred activity time for you. If you have six negative comments in the same day, that adds up to 60 minutes' loss of privileges. So at home, you would have 20 minutes of preferred activity time that evening. Then the next day is a whole new day to try to earn more preferred activity time. "

4. Describe how and when the student should mark the chart, giving examples of appropriate and inappropriate behavior:

66 *Your chart will stay on your desk while you are in class. At any time that you believe you are working diligently on your schoolwork, behaving appropriately in class, or interacting appropriately with other people, you may write a positive comment for yourself. However, if you are off task or not behaving appropriately, you will need to write that on your chart also.* **99**

5. Explain the role the student's parents will play:

66 *Each day I will make a copy of your chart for you to take home and have your parents sign. Your parents understand the chart system and will follow through with reward time at home. You will need to return the signed chart to me the next day.* **99**

If the sheet is not turned in, find out why. You may need to talk with parents. A student should not be punished for a parent's problem.

Consequences could be loss of preferred activity time at school, and rewards could be those that other children get when they behave appropriately, such as extra recess time and additional time for games and reading.

Independent Practice

The student will soon understand the process and take responsibility for the chart. This does not mean that close monitoring is not needed. Monitoring will be needed for many months to make this system work.

Closure

It may take many months for students to change their behavior. Talk with the student daily about the progress that he or she is making. Have the student help you create a chart that shows the progress made, identify areas that still need work, and set goals for the next day.

Gina's Classroom Experience

I have adopted the behavior chart in my third-grade classroom, and it works great! I believe that the students who are having trouble controlling themselves gain a sense of control from maintaining their own chart. It is short term enough that they are continually aware of the consequences and rewards waiting at the end of their chart. Rather than create a new chart, I use my classroom schedule, which is easy to reproduce. The students track themselves all day long with happy or sad faces. I had one student who was very excited when he realized that he had one morning full of happy faces. He told me that he was going to try very hard to have a "happy face afternoon," too. I thought this was great in helping him realize his progress and set a goal for the rest of the day. Now he is working on happy face weeks!

Evaluation

Keep the charts and record the progress.

Reflection

- Ask the student to share examples of how he or she reached the goals of this lesson. This could be an oral discussion or a writing assignment.

- Discuss with the student any aspects of flow that he or she experiences and add the information to the class flow chart (see page 5). Have the student write entries in his or her flow journal as well (see page 7). Young children could draw instead of write. Draw the student's attention to the fact that when experiencing flow, he or she is usually behaving appropriately.

Extension

Use the last 10 to 15 minutes of the day or of class as "choice time" for students who have behaved well and completed schoolwork. Students might choose from puzzles, card games, reading, drawing, writing, and other such activities. For other students, this might be a time to catch up on work or write about plans for improved behavior the next day.

Teacher's Record of Student Progress

Student's name: _____

Date	# of appropriate behaviors	# of inappropriate behaviors

Student Behavior Chart

Dear Parents,

Thank you for your support of the school's efforts regarding your child's behavior. Here is the way the system works. Each appropriate behavior is worth 10 minutes of preferred activity time. Each inappropriate behavior (worth 10 minutes) is subtracted from the amount of preferred time the student has earned for the day. Please sign your name at the bottom of the chart to indicate that you have followed through with the appropriate amount of reward or consequence time for your child, who should return the chart to school tomorrow.

Student's name: _____   Date: _____

Appropriate Behaviors
C = Cooperative
G = Good work
E = Excellent work
W = Works well
GA = Great attitude

Inappropriate Behaviors
T   = Talking or disruptive
OT = Off task
R   = Rude
AG = Arguing or aggressive
H   = Hitting or hurting others

Time	Appropriate Behavior	Inappropriate Behavior
8:30		
8:45		
9:00		
9:15		
9:30		
9:45		
10:00		
10:15		
10:30		
10:45		
11:00		
11:15		
11:30		
11:45		
12:00		
12:15		
12:30		
12:45		
1:00		
1:15		
1:30		
1:45		
2:00		
2:15		
2:30		
2:45		
Totals		

Active Learning: Increasing Flow in the Classroom, © 2006 Crown House Publishing Company Ltd. • www.crownhouse.co.uk

Parent's signature:_____   Date: _____

Part Two

Active Learning in the Arts

Chapter 4
Movement Arts

Kinesphere and Jumble Jive

— Gail N. Herman —

Movement Arts

The movement arts tap into the emotions and attention of students. Movement activities are a way to provide a break from intense, quiet, seated tasks. The movement arts help students develop discipline, cooperation, body agility, balance, flexibility, and strength. Many athletes take courses in movement, ballet, other types of dance, and even mime to develop their kinesthetic abilities and skills.

Movement activities can become part of the daily routine for the entire class. They provide a way to channel student energy in a positive way. These activities get and keep students' attention.

Materials

- ☐ drum
- ☐ camera
- ☐ student flow journals (see page 7)

Preparation

1. If you do not have access to a drum, create one or drum on an everyday object such as a coffee can or even your desk. Some teachers even do this activity without a drum.

2. Practice the movements described in Guided Practice for defining your kinesphere before demonstrating this to students.

3. Clear enough space for all students to move freely at least an arm's distance from each other.

 ## Getting Students Excited about the Topic

1. Share the aims with students, as described in the Measurable Learning Objectives section above. Explain that you will show them how to create their own physical spaces, called *kinespheres,* in which they will explore shapes and directions within their own personal space.

2. Lead the class in a warm-up. Have students follow along as you walk in place, slowly work your way to a jog, then slow back down to a walk.

Guided Practice

1. Ask students to find a self-space so that when their arms are extended, they touch no one. Tell them that this space is their *kinesphere.*

2. As you discuss the word "sphere," put one foot in front of you in a lunge position and stretch your arms forward, miming a wall in front of you.

3. Pull your foot back to the center, then lunge that foot out to the side and return to the center. Lunge the other foot out to the other side, then in front, then behind you, in turn, so that students can see the boundaries of the space that is each of theirs. Point out that they must keep one foot in the center of the kinesphere.

4. Discuss how a kinesphere becomes smaller when objects or people are near.

Independent Practice

1. Encourage the students to stretch with you. Tell them to focus their eyes in the direction they are stretching as you call out the direction: up (go up on toes), side, other side, front right corner, front left corner, and so on in every direction.

   Note: To stretch backward, students should keep one foot planted in the center and place one foot behind them, stretching one arm way back while looking at it.

2. Next, tell them to stretch in each direction as you beat the drum and call a direction. If you do not have a drum, you can clap or snap.

Jumble Jive

1. Tell students that in the next activity, the Jumble Jive, they can make their own stretching shapes in any direction they choose.

2. Teach them to clap and say "1–2–3-4-5" to this rhythm: slow, slow, quick, quick, quick.

3. Teach them to *patch* (brush the top of their hips) and clap, alternately. Arms are always bent at the elbow and swing back and forth simultaneously. First, both hands brush the top of the hips, going back, then swing up to clap at about chest level.

4. Next, teach them to patch and clap to this chant:

   Jumble jive, jumble jive
   What can you do to the count of five? 1–2–3-4-5

What to say	Motion to make
Jum-	With arms bent at elbow, brush top of hips with both palms
ble	Swing arms up and clap once
Jive	Swing arms down and brush top of hips with both palms
Jum-	Clap
ble	Brush hips
Jive	Clap
What	Brush
can	Clap
you	Brush
do	Clap
to	Brush
the	Clap
count	Brush
of	Clap
five?	Brush
one	Clap (slow)
two	Brush (slow)
three	Clap (quick)
four	Brush (quick)
five	Clap (quick)

5. Divide the class into groups of five. Each person in the group takes a number from one to five.

6. Everyone says the chant together. At the end of the chant, each person will make a stretching shape as you call the numbers. As you call "one," the first student in each group makes a stretching shape. Then as you call "two," the second student makes a shape near the first, and so on for each of the group members. If a group has four members, one student must go twice. If a group has six members, two students will have to go at the same time.

7. Ask them to try to make shapes going in different directions than the people who went before them. That way the total group tableau will have contrasts and look more interesting.

8. After several rounds, ask each group to name its tableau. This allows students to see that you are enjoying their creativity. If they get stuck, ask them how they feel or tell them how they look to you. Examples of names: butter churn, creative shapes, opposite machine, aliens, trees, circus, junkyard cars, at the beach, the ball game, an accident, clowns, cheers, and so on.

9. Then ask them to use alliteration and original words to subtitle their group tableau.

10. Finally, take pictures of each group's shape.

Closure

Close by pointing out that they learned to explore and describe the basic elements of dance by using their bodies as instruments in a variety of ways.

Evaluation

Ask students as a group to evaluate themselves on the following points:

- Students experienced proper body positioning (placement and alignment—balancing, standing, moving).

- Students explored, defined, and maintained personal space.

- Students explored shapes, angles, lines, curves, and directions. (forward, backward, left, right, etc.)

- Students developed the ability to produce spontaneous movement from various stimuli and create various movements through improvisation.

- Students represented ideas, objects, and feelings using movement.

- Students explored various kinesthetic sensations (internal stimuli).

Reflection

- Ask students to share examples of how they reached the goals of this lesson. This could be an oral discussion or a writing assignment.

- Discuss with your students any aspects of flow that they experienced and add the information to the class flow chart (see page 5). Then ask students to make entries in their flow journals (see page 7). Young children could draw instead of write.

Extension

Silent kinesphere: Once students have been introduced to the kinesphere, ask a student to be the silent movement leader. All students follow the rules of the kinesphere while also following the leader in absolute silence. For example, leaders might walk, run, or jump in place. They might move their arms like robots, go up on tiptoe, or sweep down low. When you signal with a clap or a snap, the leader selects someone else to lead.

Chapter 5
Thor and the Missing Hammer

Introducing Drama to Young Students

— Pat Hollingsworth —

Thor and the Missing Hammer

When students are introduced to drama at an early age, they learn to be comfortable in front of an audience. Dramatic movement also provides students with legitimate opportunities to use their energy. Allowing students to move from quiet, seated work activities to activities that involve movement helps maintain mental alertness. This change provides a physical reprieve for students that helps them enjoy and get more out of their schoolwork (Smith 2005).

Each time you read a book in the classroom, you have an opportunity to introduce movement and drama to your students. Not only does movement make the story come alive, it also helps students remember the material. This lesson uses the story "Thor and the Missing Hammer" to illustrate how to get students involved in drama during reading. At appropriate junctures in the story, examples of how to incorporate drama and movement are included. This method can be used with any story you read to students. Drama and movement can greatly enhance attention to detail and memory of story content while keeping students' bodies and minds active.

Materials

- ☐ "Thor and the Missing Hammer" (page 35)
- ☐ Drama Self-Evaluation (page 40)
- ☐ costumes and simple props (such as scarves, capes, old tablecloths, vests, toy hammers, and crowns)
- ☐ small classroom bell or other noisemaker
- ☐ student flow journals (see page 7)

Supplementary Materials

☐ small basket or other container for costumes and simple props

☐ fiction and nonfiction books about thunder and lightning (such as other folktales as well as basic explanatory books for the age group)

Preparation

1. Practice reading the story aloud, including the cues to dramatize, so that you are able to read dramatically and smoothly during the lesson. (Note that for the Independent Practice, you will ring a bell or use some other cue instead of reading the "dramatize" sections.)

2. For the Independent Practice, prepare a container (such as a basket) of enough costumes and props for each student to have at least one during any dramatization.

3. If you have not already read chapter 4, review it and be prepared to describe a kinesphere to students (or use a different word when describing self-space to students in this lesson).

4. Clear enough space for students to move freely while acting out the story.

 ## Getting Students Excited about the Topic

1. Getting students excited for this activity is easy. Most children love to pretend. Play up on their sense of adventure and exploration:

   > **"** *Do you like to pretend? Do you like to make up stories and take parts in them? I know some of you create interesting games on the playground, such as being construction workers, superheroes, and space travelers. Today we are going to get into our kinespheres and do some exploring.* **"**

2. Explain the aims of the lesson, so that students understand the goals and keep them in mind throughout, then tell them that you will read a story, asking them to act out parts of it as you read. For example, you might say,

   > **"** *We are going to start doing some drama in class as we read a story called "Thor and the Missing Hammer." I will read a few paragraphs and then ask you to dramatize that part of the story. Later you will dramatize the story without me telling you how to do it.* **"**

Guided Practice

1. Warm up with a few simple drama techniques so that students are able to freeze on command and create and remain within their own kinesphere (personal space):

   ❝Before we begin, we need to practice drama in a way that will be fun but won't get out of control. First, let's practice our freeze technique. I will ask everyone to stand and do some movements. Then as soon as I say, "Freeze," you are to freeze both your bodies and your mouths.

   Now everyone stand and stay in your kinesphere. Let's first practice moving in our own kinespheres. Remember that your kinesphere will stay in place and not touch anyone else's space. Now pretend that you are jogging in the park. Next, imagine that you are sitting before a nice big fire. Freeze. Good job! All of you stayed in your kinespheres and froze at the appropriate time.❞

2. Next, introduce the story with a few major elements, such as the origin of the myth, what a myth is, and what this myth attempts to explain. For example:

   ❝The story we will read and dramatize today is a myth about Norse gods and goddesses. What country would that be? Yes, it is a story from Norway. A myth often tries to explain something. This one is called "Thor and the Missing Hammer."

   Thor is the Norse god of thunder and lightning. The myth says that the rumbling wheels of Thor's chariot are the thunder we hear during a storm, and the flash of Thor's hammer is lightning. We know that these do not really cause thunder and lightning, but it is still an interesting story. Later we will do some research into the real causes of thunder and lightning.❞

Thor and the Missing Hammer: A Norse Legend

ADAPTED BY PAT HOLLINGSWORTH

King Odin and Queen Frigg lived in a beautiful palace called Valhalla in a cold land. Their mighty children, Thor and Balder, lived at Valhalla with them.

Dramatize: *Pretend to be King Odin or Queen Frigg sitting on a throne at Valhalla.*

Each evening, two ravens named Thought and Memory sat on King Odin's shoulders. Each day they flew around the world to gather information for King Odin. In the evening they would return to sit on his shoulders and give him the nightly news. Often the ravens would bring news of the Frost Giants, the dreaded enemies of the kingdom. One night the ravens whispered, "The Frost Giants are going to steal Thor's hammer." But no one was listening.

Dramatize: *Be one of the ravens. Fly out into the world then back to the palace. Whisper in King Odin's ear that the Frost Giants are going to steal Thor's hammer.*

At King Odin's feet sat two fierce wolves to protect him. He would toss them pieces of roasted boar meat to keep them satisfied.

Dramatize: *Be a fierce wolf sitting at King Odin's feet. Grab a piece of meat as King Odin throws it to you.*

Thor, the thunderer, was the strongest of all King Odin's children. Thor traveled across the sky in his chariot pulled by mighty goats. He was never without his great hammer, which he carried in his hand. Thor made the heavens thunder as he crossed the skies. He was constantly in battle with his enemies, the Frost Giants.

Dramatize: *Pretend that you are Thor making thunder as you cross the skies in your chariot pulled by goats.*

One day Thor could not find his hammer. He searched everywhere he could think to search. In the evening the ravens told him that the hammer had been stolen by the Frost Giants. If the beautiful Freya, goddess of love and spring, would marry the Frost King, the hammer would be returned to Thor.

Freya said, "Never, never, never will I marry the Frost King. That would mean the end of love and springtime." All of Freya's lovely attendants agreed and repeated after her, "Never, never, never."

Dramatize: *Tell Thor that you will never marry the Frost King.*

Thor was at a loss as to what to do, until Loki, the king of mischief, came with an answer. Loki and the people in his kingdom had been working on a solution.

Loki said, "Thor, you must dress to look like a bride and pretend to be Freya." All his advisers agreed, "Yes, Thor must dress to look like Freya."

Thor was not convinced, "Loki, that is a preposterous idea. I will not dress like a bride. I will never, ever, ever dress to look like a bride."

"Then you will never see your hammer again," Loki said. All of Loki's advisers agreed and said, "Then you will never see your hammer again."

Thor finally realized that Loki was right. "I have no other choice. I cannot be the thunder god without my mighty hammer."

Dramatize: *Be Loki giving Thor advice.*

So Thor shaved his mustache; then he dressed in a beautiful bridal dress and traveled far north to the land of the Frost Giants. Thor's face was covered with veils so that no one could recognize him.

The Frost Giants had prepared a banquet for the king and his bride. Thor seemed to have fooled the Frost Giants with his disguise—that is, until Thor began to eat. When he ate an entire boar, four ducks, and three hens, the Frost King became suspicious. Clever Loki quickly made up an excuse: "King, your bride is very hungry because of the long journey. She was so anxious to get here that she did not stop to eat."

Dramatize: *Be Thor taking the long journey to the icy home of the Frost Giants. When you arrive at the palace, you forget that you are supposed to be Freya and begin to eat a huge meal.*

At long last the Frost King brought out Thor's hammer and handed it to Loki. The moment Thor spied the hammer, he threw off his bridal disguise and grabbed it. Thor and Loki made a quick exit with the hammer and were off as fast as lightning.

Dramatize: *Be Thor as he sees the hammer, throws off the disguise, grabs the hammer, and takes off.*

Active Learning: Increasing Flow in the Classroom, © 2006 Crown House Publishing Company Ltd. • www.crownhouse.co.uk

Independent Practice 1

1. Plan a regular time to have drama, perhaps several times a week, after students have been working intensely on another subject, such as math.

2. The next time you read the story, do not read the "dramatize" sections—ring a small bell instead. Each time drama takes place in the class, the students should take more responsibility for the words and actions.

> **❝** *Today when we have drama, I will pause briefly at various places in the story and ring our small bell. That will be your cue to dramatize the section I have just read to you. Remember to stay in your kinesphere and freeze when signaled to do so.* **❞**

Independent Practice 2

1. The next step is full dramatization of the play. Designate five locations in your room for five groups of students. It is helpful to leave an open space in the middle for the chariot group. Divide the class into the following groups:

   - King Odin and Queen Frigg's palace group also includes Balder, Thor, the ravens, and the wolves
   - Frost Giants' palace group includes Frost King, Queen, Princes, and Princesses
   - Spring goddess Freya's palace group also includes many lovely attendants
   - Loki's kingdom group includes his helpers
   - Thor's chariot group includes the wild, fierce goats (thunder, lightning, the chariot, and a hammer could also be parts, if you wish to be imaginative)

2. There are parts for 10 to 30 students. Tell them that they will have the opportunity to play a different part during the next drama time. All students will get a chance to play all parts they wish to try. It does not matter if several students wish to be the same character. There can be more than one Thor or Freya, for example, playing the part at the same time. You could divide the class yourself or ask students which parts they want to play:

> **❝** *During drama today, you will be divided into five groups. How many will that be for each group? Okay, raise your hand if you want to be in Loki's kingdom. If you do not get your chance today to be in your favorite group, you will have many other chances. I want everyone to have the chance to play his or her favorite parts.* **❞**

3. As soon as you have selected students for a group, ask everyone to move to their designated locations in the room.

4. When all students have been selected and are in their designated locations, begin reading the story, pausing or using the bell when you want the students to speak and act.

Independent Practice 3

1. Continue to practice the play a couple of times a week, letting everyone have a chance to play every part they wish. As time progresses, students usually decide on the parts they most like to play. Get the students to make their decisions and write down the names, making sure every part is covered.

2. At this point, you may wish to have a performance for the parents. Be sure they know that it is a very short, probably 10-minute, play. Send a note home telling parents when the play will be and what part their child will play. Ask them to devise a simple costume for the student to wear on the day of the play.

3. Give parents some idea of how to create a costume. Long skirts are good for queens, princesses, goddesses, and brides; gray sweatsuits for wolves; white for Frost Giants; and black for ravens. Kings and queens wear crowns.

4. Keep the event low key. Having the play during the first few minutes of class usually draws a good audience and does not put much pressure on the parents or children. The goal is for the children to enjoy presenting a play for an audience. This is just the first step in learning to be comfortable in front of spectators.

Closure

After the play, ask students to describe what they liked best about giving the performance. Remind them of how much each of them has learned.

Evaluation

Have students who can read and write fill out the Drama Self-Evaluation on page 40. For other students, go through the questions orally with the group.

Reflection

- Ask students to share examples of how they reached the goals of this lesson. This could be an oral discussion or a writing assignment.

- Discuss with your students any aspects of flow that they experienced and add the information to the class flow chart (see page 5). Then ask students to make entries in their flow journals (see page 7). Young children could draw instead of write.

Extension

- Have students research the real causes of thunder and lightning.

- Have students write their own myths to explain natural phenomena.

- Have students draw pictures of storms.

- Read myths from other countries for the students to dramatize.

Drama Self-Evaluation

Name: _____ Date: _____

1. How comfortable were you in dramatizing stories?

    A. Very
    B. Somewhat
    C. Not comfortable

2. How well did you remember the sequence of the story?

    A. Very well
    B. Okay
    C. Not well

3. How well did you do in presenting the play?

    A. Very well
    B. Okay
    C. Not well

4. What did you do best?

_____

_____

_____

5. What would you do differently next time?

_____

_____

_____

Active Learning: Increasing Flow in the Classroom, © 2006 Crown House Publishing Company Ltd. • www.crownhouse.co.uk

Chapter 6

The Story of the Trojan Horse

Drama for Elementary Students
— Gina Lewis —

Grades: 1–6

Time Frame Options

- Day 1: 30 minutes
- Day 2: 1 hour
- Subsequent days: 1 hour daily

Measurable Learning Objectives

Share these aims with students:

- Day 1: Students will become familiar with a historical event by hearing and reading the story of the Trojan Horse.
- Day 2: Students will write and memorize lines to fit the story.
- Subsequent days: Students will invent acting and movement to fit the story.
- Students will create masks, costumes, and sets to fit the play.

The Story of the Trojan Horse

D rama is an excellent device for the active learning of history. Once students are actively involved in costume, setting, and dialogue, the stories of history become real and easier to retain in long-term memory. Feel free to improvise and modify this play to fit your classroom. The story "Ulysses and the Trojan Horse" from the SAILS curriculum *Ancient Greece* workbook (Hollingsworth 2000) served as a guide for this play. Read it to your students to give them an idea of the sequence and flow to follow. Students will be able to create the play almost independently following the guide of that book. The concept can apply to other historical periods as well: Students could improvise a Lewis and Clark skit, act out a play based on Paul Revere's ride, or adapt a familiar fairy tale during a Middle Ages unit.

The greatest thing to remember in teaching drama is to be flexible and let the play evolve. The students are much more interested when they know that their ideas and contributions will be considered and developed into the play.

Materials

- ☐ costume materials (sheets, skirts, vests, fabric)
- ☐ cardboard or posterboard for sets
- ☐ pencils and paper for all students
- ☐ markers or paint
- ☐ miscellaneous craft supplies such as scissors, glue, tape, string, and so forth
- ☐ "Ulysses and the Trojan Horse" (page 45)
- ☐ Sequence of Events (page 44)
- ☐ student flow journals (see page 7)

Supplementary Materials

- ☐ tagboard for masks
- ☐ simple props, such as toy ships and arrows
- ☐ musical instruments for sound effects
- ☐ camera
- ☐ scrapbook

Preparation

1. Read the play starting on page 45 to become familiar with it.

2. Enlarge the Sequence of Events (page 44) onto 11" x 17" paper (or larger, if possible) and post it where the entire class can see it.

3. Gather the materials, with the idea in mind of keeping the set and costumes simple so that students focus primarily on the acting and the story.

 ## Getting Students Excited about the Topic

1. Begin by describing the lesson and sharing the aims (see Measurable Learning Objectives). Tell students about the play you are about to read and ask them to think about the characters, props, sets, and costumes they would need to present it.

   ❝ *Has anyone ever heard of Achilles? Or Odysseus? How about the Trojan War? I am going to read 'Ulysses and the Trojan Horse,' and I want you to visualize this as a play. I need each one of you to consider the different characters from the story and think about the props and sets that might be required.* **❞**

2. Read the play aloud.

Sequence of Events

SCENE 1

- Helen is stolen by Paris.

- Ulysses, Achilles, and Greek soldiers follow after.

SCENE 2

- The Greeks and the Trojans begin a war.

- Achilles is shot in the heel.

- Ulysses decides to build the horse.

SCENE 3

- Greeks build the horse.

- Greeks enter the horse.

- Horse is pushed up to the city gates.

SCENE 4

- Trojans see Greeks sailing away and celebrate.

SCENE 5

- Trojans find the horse.

SCENE 6

- Laocoon throws spear at horse.

SCENE 7

- When Sinon is captured, he lies about the horse.

SCENE 8

- Trojans tear down their wall and celebrate.

SCENE 9

- Greeks sneak out of horse, capture the city, and rescue Helen.

Active Learning: Increasing Flow in the Classroom, © 2006 Crown House Publishing Company Ltd. • www.crownhouse.co.uk

Ulysses and the Trojan Horse
BY PATRICIA HOLLINGSWORTH
RETOLD BY GINA LEWIS

CAST OF CHARACTERS

In order of appearance:

Helen, *Greek queen* (Helen can have handmaidens around her if you need extra parts.)

Paris, *prince of Troy*

Achilles, *Greek soldier*

Ulysses/Odysseus (oh-DIS-ee-us), the Wanderer, *Greek general*

Greek soldiers (as many as you need)

Trojan soldiers (as many as you need)

Laocoon (Lay-awk-uh-wahn), *wise Trojan*

Sinon (Sigh-non), *Greek soldier*

Priam (Pri-um), *king of Troy*

Narrator (I have used up to four narrators.)

SCENE 1

The war between the Greeks and the Trojans began when Paris, a Trojan prince, stole a beautiful Greek queen named Helen. The Greeks decided to fight to get Helen back. Greek soldiers sailed to Troy with General Achilles and General Ulysses, also known as Odysseus, the Wanderer.

Stage notes: *Props of ships are fun here. Helen can be in a chair on one side of the stage and act very distressed when Paris pulls her to a chair on the other side of the stage.*

SCENE 2

During the long war, Paris shot Achilles in the heel and killed him. The Greeks were becoming discouraged. For nearly ten years, the Greeks had been fighting the Trojans. Just as the Greek soldiers were about to give up, General Ulysses had an idea that would win the war. "We are going to build a huge wooden horse."

Stage notes: *Achilles limping across the stage with an arrow taped to his heel is comical. Be sure that all the Greek soldiers are looking discouraged and downcast. When the soldiers are fighting, they should use very slow, very exaggerated fighting movements without actually touching one another. Remember that they are fighting outside the gates of Troy. You may want to have the gates as a prop, or they can be imaginary.*

SCENE 3

The soldiers grumbled, "A wooden horse can't help us win the war." But they did as Ulysses told them. Then late one night, Ulysses ordered that the horse be quietly moved close to the walls of the city of Troy. Ulysses and most of the soldiers climbed into the horse where they could not be seen and did not make a sound.

Stage notes: *The horse can be made of cardboard that the students stand behind, with their legs and faces still visible. A cloth horse could work as well. Remind them that everyone is looking at them even though they are inside the horse. It is important that they continue acting.*

SCENE 4

The next part of Ulysses' plan was to make the Trojans think that the Greeks had given up and gone home. In the morning, the Trojans woke up to see the Greek ships sailing away. They began to shout, "The Greeks have given up and are sailing home." They did not know that most of the ships were hidden at nearby islands.

Stage notes: *Have the Trojans partying and singing, "The Greeks are gone! The Greeks are gone! And that's the way, uh huh, uh huh, we like it, uh huh, uh huh!"*

SCENE 5

The Trojans were so delighted that the Greeks were gone that they ran out the gates of the city. Just outside the city wall, they found the huge wooden horse. The people of Troy began to ask questions, "What is this thing that the Greeks have left behind? What is it for? Why did they leave it? What should we do with it?"

Stage notes: *The soldiers inside the horse might hold their mouths to keep quiet.*

SCENE 6

A wise man, named Laocoon, told the people to destroy the horse. He said, "I fear the Greeks even when they offer gifts." Then he threw his spear and hit the wooden horse. Inside the horse, the Greeks could hear everything that was happening, but they did not make a sound.

Stage notes: *The soldiers inside the horse might continue to hold their mouths and look concerned.*

SCENE 7

The next moment a Greek named Sinon was found by the Trojans. Sinon pretended to be angry with Ulysses. He said, "Because Ulysses left me here to die, I will tell you the secret of the wooden horse. The horse was made so large that it would not fit through your city gates. The Greeks knew if you were to get the horse inside the city walls, it would mean your victory. This horse was to be a gift to the powerful goddess Athena. Whoever has the horse has the favor of Athena." Laocoon again tried to warn the Trojans about the horse. But no one was listening.

SCENE 8

The people of Troy began to shout, "The horse belongs to us. Bring the Trojan horse into the city." But the gates of the city were too small to allow the huge horse to enter. "Tear down part of the wall. We must have our Trojan horse. It is our trophy for winning the war with the Greeks." So the Trojans tore down part of the wall that protected their city to make way for a wooden horse that would mean their downfall.

Stage notes: *Have Priam, king of Troy, say the part about "Tear down the wall." Students could make up additional lines for him.*

SCENE 9

The Trojans spent the day and evening celebrating their victory over the Greeks. Finally, everyone in the city slept—everyone except the Greeks. Ulysses and his men quietly slipped out of the horse. In a short time, the Greeks gained control of the city of Troy. The beautiful queen Helen was found. She and the other Greeks boarded their ships to return to their homeland. This was the end of the war between the Greeks and the Trojans.

Stage notes: *Have the Greeks in one color and the Trojans in another to easily identify the two factions, because who is on which side can become confusing. Have the students mime tying up the Trojans rather than any violent killing acts. At the end, all join hands and bow.*

Adapted from *Classical Greece,* SAILS, © 2000, reprinted by permission of University School at the University of Tulsa, www.uschool.utulsa.edu.

Guided Practice

1. After you finish reading the play, explain to students that they will create a play of their own, based on the one you just read.

2. Describe the different roles students will need to fill: narrators, actors, and set managers. You might add other roles, such as costume designers and prop managers. Have students write down their top three choices for the part or role they want, and tell them that they will get one of their three selections. (This method works best at the elementary level. Try-outs can be stressful and unduly time consuming.) For example, you might say,

   "*Creating a play requires many different talents and abilities. To perform this play we need narrators, actors, and set managers. Think about which area you would like to work in and write your top three selections on a sheet of paper. I will organize these and give each of you one of your three selections. If you do not get the part that you really want, there will be another play or two before the year is over.***"**

3. Point out the Sequence of Events posted as a reminder of the nine scenes in the story and have students break up into groups based on their roles. For example:

   "*By now you are all familiar with the Greek story of the Trojan Horse, and each of you has received the part you will have in the play. I have placed all nine scenes of the story on the board to remind us of the sequence we are following. Everyone has a job to do. If you are a narrator or an actor, you need to write and memorize your lines. Set managers need to discuss the set, make your decisions, and begin working on the set.***"**

Independent Practice

1. The narrators and actors should produce their lines, and the set managers should produce their sketches for the setting. Leave costumes and props up to the individuals and have the Greeks in one color and the Trojans in another. During this time, you might help students with writing the dialogue (if your students are young) or simply be available to advise and answer questions.

2. Discuss the lines and sketches as a class and do a run-through. Rehearsals are imperative but should be kept short. Many short rehearsals are better than a few grueling long ones. If you keep the play short and simple, rehearsals are not a big hassle. Rehearse at the front of the classroom with no props or sets many times before the actual dress rehearsals. While the actors and narrators are rehearsing, the set people are building the set. A couple of dress rehearsals before the actual performance are necessary for the actors to become accustomed to their props and costumes and for the set managers to get used to changing scenes. Elaborate sets and set changes are not necessary.

3. Students perform the play for other classes, parents, or the school while you take pictures.

Closure

- Create a classroom scrapbook or bulletin board of pictures and souvenirs from the play.

- Have the students write summaries of their experiences and the important things they learned during the play.

Evaluation

Have students complete the Play Evaluation (pages 50–51) to demonstrate comprehension. (See the answer sheet on page 52.)

Reflection

- Ask students to share examples of how they reached the goals of this lesson. This could be an oral discussion or a writing assignment.

- Discuss with your students any aspects of flow that they experienced and add the information to the class flow chart (see page 5). Then ask students to make entries in their flow journals (see page 7).

Extension

- Students could perform the play in nursing homes or retirement centers to benefit the community and teach the students about community service.

- Students could read other texts or watch movies about the Trojan War.

- Students could study maps of ancient Greece and Troy.

Play Evaluation

Name: _____ Date: _____

Part 1

Fill in the blanks to answer the questions.

1. Which two groups were fighting this war? _____ and _____

2. Who was the Greek queen? _____

3. What was the name of the Greek general? _____

4. What was the name of the Trojan general? _____

5. What great Greek soldier was shot in the heel? _____

6. The Greeks built a _____ to trick the Trojans.

7. The Greeks traveled to Troy on _____

8. _____ warned the Trojans not to accept the gift of the horse.

9. _____ was left behind by the Greeks to help trick the Trojans.

10. What goddess was mentioned in the play? _____

Part 2

Put the following events in order using numbers 1–9.

_____ Sinon is captured and lies about the horse.

_____ Achilles is shot in the heel.

_____ The Trojans find the horse.

_____ Paris steals Helen.

_____ The Greeks sneak out of the horse and capture the city of Troy and rescue Helen.

_____ The Trojans see the Greeks sailing away.

_____ The horse is pushed up to the city gates.

_____ The Trojans tear down their wall and celebrate.

_____ Laocoon throws his spear at the horse.

Active Learning: Increasing Flow in the Classroom, © 2006 Crown House Publishing Company Ltd. • www.crownhouse.co.uk

Part 3

In the space below, draw and label a scene from the play.

Part 4

Extra credit: Who wrote the original story about the Trojan horse? _____

Play Evaluation Answer Sheet

Part 1

1. Greeks and Trojans
2. Helen
3. Ulysses or Odysseus
4. Paris
5. Achilles
6. a wooden horse
7. ships
8. Laocoon
9. Sinon
10. Athena

Part 2

7 Sinon is captured and lies about the horse.

2 Achilles is shot in the heel.

5 The Trojans find the horse.

1 Paris steals Helen.

9 The Greeks sneak out of the horse, capture the city of Troy, and rescue Helen.

4 The Trojans see the Greeks sailing away.

3 The horse is pushed up to the city gates.

8 The Trojans tear down their wall and celebrate.

6 Laocoon throws his spear at the horse.

Part 3

Answers will vary.

Part 4

Homer

Chapter 7

Make Social Studies Come Alive

Drama for Middle School Students

— Marilyn Cox —

Grades: 5–8

Time Frame Options

- Day 1: 30 minutes
- Day 2: 1 hour
- Subsequent days (as needed): 1 hour

Measurable Learning Objectives

Share these aims with students:

- Students will learn critical facts related to the particular event.
- Students will research the period and characters in the play.
- Students will analyze plot sequence.
- Students will learn about clothing of the period.
- Students will learn to face the audience, speak clearly, keep action moving, project their voices, and be aware of their own and others' bodies.
- Students will learn to present ideas and to listen to others' ideas.
- Students will present a play to an audience.

Make Social Studies Come Alive

In his research, Csikszentmihalyi has found that students rate history as the least engaging of school subjects (Scherer 2002). Creating plays based on history is an excellent way to solve that problem. Students not only learn the facts, they understand and remember them longer. Plays are especially helpful to kinesthetic learners. Acquiring knowledge through reading and research is more exciting when there is a reason beyond studying for a test. Students also experience working together creatively. Plays bring excitement and creativity to history because there is no right or wrong way to do them.

Materials

- ☐ Three to four sheets self-sticking easel paper or large pieces of butcher paper and tape
- ☐ felt-tip pen
- ☐ paper and pencil for each student to take notes
- ☐ simple costumes and props (related to period of study)
- ☐ student flow journals (see page 7)

Supplementary Materials

- ☐ history textbook
- ☐ children's and young adult historical fiction and nonfiction (such as *The Courage of Sarah Noble, Phoebe the Spy, Johnny Tremain,* and *The Secret Soldier*)
- ☐ reference books such as The Timetables of History by Bernard Grun (students can look up by year what was new in areas such as music, literature, inventions, and daily life)
- ☐ encyclopedias for research on topic and period
- ☐ Internet access for research on topic and period

Preparation

1. Clear enough space in the room for students to perform skits, mini-dramas, or a play (depending on which part of the Guided Practice or Independent Practice you are doing on a particular day).

2. For the Independent Practice, set up an easel or tape up the butcher paper in preparation for brainstorming a plot.

 ## Getting Students Excited about the Topic

1. Motivate students by explaining that they will be using drama to act out what they are learning about history. Share the objectives of the lesson so that students understand and feel invested in reaching the goals. You might start by saying,

   66 *History is much more exciting when you get to know the people you study. We are going to bring history to life by using the facts we learn to put words in people's mouths and create a drama.* **99**

2. Next, describe the important elements in the historical play, such as choosing a person or event; including details from the period to add authenticity; and considering how people spoke at the time when creating dialogue:

   66 *Our job is to create a play about history in a way that will inform and entertain the audience. In a play, the story is told through action and dialogue. We will decide what the audience needs to know by writing a plot line and choosing characters to tell our story. First, we must learn about the person or event that our play will be about, including information about what was going on in the world at the time to add interest. We are creating historical fiction, so we must be as historically correct as possible while making up dialogue.* **99**

3. Explain that before the class begins writing full plays, students will practice improvising scenes, taking turns to act out the scene in different ways. After each improvisation, the class will discuss what worked well and what should be added to be sure the audience will understand the story.

4. Provide basic guidelines for the improvised scenes before students begin:

   - The audience needs to know who the characters are, so students should say the names of the characters they are speaking to at least once during the improvisation.

   - The audience needs to know when and where the events take place, so students should be sure to include these details in the action or dialogue.

■ Each line of dialogue should be important in building the story.

MAKING HISTORY!

■ Before beginning a scene, students should think about the characters they are playing. If playing real people, students should learn what they can about them and include this information in their lines. If portraying imaginary people, students should decide how they want to play the person and develop a character with a personality that fits the period.

■ Students should speak clearly and face the audience (when not facing another character).

Guided Practice

1. **Weekly informal skits:** When students have an opportunity to dramatize what they have learned, they will be more excited about the content and will remember it better. A good rhythm is to cover the material in class, then divide students into four or five groups, giving them three to five minutes to create a one- or two-minute skit to share with the class. Remind them that it must have a beginning, a middle, and an end. The planning and presentations should take only about 15 minutes total. This can be done once or more a week as a way to introduce students to doing plays and skits.

2. **Minidramas:** After practicing with skits, but before the whole class creates a play, students learn the playwriting and performance processes

by working in groups on four or five minidramas throughout the semester. After reading several chapters in a history book, each group of four or five students is assigned a different event from those studied. In one class period, they create and practice a short play that they perform for the class. This gives them experience working together, and they get ideas from watching the other groups. Using a few class periods each semester on minidramas solidifies learning and creates excitement.

Independent Practice

1. The class decides on the topic for a play to be put on only once that year. Students make suggestions from the period they are studying, and the class discusses the ideas, then votes. For your first play, you may want to use children's or young adult historical fiction as a guide, such as the ideas listed in the Supplementary Materials section on page 54.

2. Create the plot line for the play with the class. Write each plot point on a large easel pad with self-sticking sheets or on butcher paper taped to the wall so that you can reference it as the play progresses. A plot line divided into three scenes works well for a short play.

3. Discuss and note what characters will be needed at each step. Guide the class toward creating enough characters so that each student has a part. Assign parts at this point or during the improvisation to follow.

4. Students begin with the first scene and improvise a variety of scenarios, with each part being played by several students. Students who are not acting in the scene should watch so that everyone can discuss what was good or what important information was left out. Assign someone to take notes so that the best ideas are not forgotten. Compliment students who remember to face the audience and speak clearly.

5. When you observe a student developing a character that really helps the story progress, assign that part to the student. The size of a part depends on the student. A secondary character could be developed into a primary character during the improvisation as the actor creates action and dialogue that help the plot progress.

6. As the class decides what works for a scene, the actors practice to make it more efficient, but few changes are made. Work on the next scene begins. Sometimes a narrator is useful to set the new scene, but encourage students to work all the information into the scene's action and dialogue.

7. Students practice each scene until the play is ready to present.

8. Provide pictures of period clothing and discuss with students inexpensive ways to create costumes. For example, in a play set in colonial or revolutionary America, sweatpants pulled up to the knee worn with knee socks, a white shirt, and a vest for male characters, and a long skirt and shawl for female characters are easy to assemble. A bit of lace at the throat and a tricorn hat from a costume shop can be added for male characters.

9. Keep props simple. You might need little more than a table and chairs.

10. Students perform the play for other students or parents.

Closure

1. Conduct a class discussion about the benefits students receive in creating and performing a play.

2. Students then write a page about how they felt the play helped them learn. As a writing prompt, ask them to use specific examples in their writing to convince you that it was a worthwhile use of class time and provided valuable learning experiences for students.

Evaluation

Use the Classroom Drama Checklist (page 59) to evaluate each student.

Reflection

■ Ask students to share examples of how they reached the goals of this lesson. This could be an oral discussion or a writing assignment.

■ Discuss with your students any aspects of flow that they experienced and add the information to the class flow chart (see page 5). Then ask students to make entries in their flow journals (see page 7).

Extension

■ Cross-curricular applications: Research and create a play about a scientist, mathematician, or author.

■ In language arts, discuss the structure of a play and the use of literary devices.

■ Use *Literature and Writing Workshop: Exploring Plays* (Jerome-Cohen 1994).

Classroom Drama Checklist

Name: _____ Date: _____

Topic: _____

Knowledge of material (0–2 points) _____

    ☐ Familiar with topic from assigned reading
    ☐ Knowledge from additional research of topic
    ☐ Knowledge from additional research of historical time period

Group dynamics (0–2 points) _____

    ☐ Group cooperation and agreement
    ☐ Everyone created
    ☐ Everyone played a part
    ☐ Individual on task
    ☐ No put-downs

Presentation (0–2 points) _____

    ☐ Organized
    ☐ Creative
    ☐ Audience engaged
    ☐ Individual faced audience and spoke clearly

Total points: _____

Scale:
6 = Excellent
5 = Very good
4 = Good
3 = Average
2 or below = Needs improvement

Chapter 8
Copland's Rodeo

An Introduction to Form in Music

— Arlene DeVries —

Copland's Rodeo

Grades: K–8

Time Frame Options

Approximately two or three 30-minute sessions

Measurable Learning Objectives

Share these aims with students:

- Students will learn to listen with appreciation to classical music.
- Students will identify the A and B sections of music.

Students can learn to enjoy classical music of the great twentieth-century American composers when they begin to understand the form in which music is put together. The ability to recognize patterns in music will also help students with pattern recognition in other subjects, such as when studying poetry, art, and math. Aaron Copland (1900–1990) was one of the first American composers to write for radio, theater, opera, ballet, and the symphony orchestra. He incorporated American folk melodies, cowboy ballads, and jazz rhythms in his classical compositions. He believed the life of art must mean something to the everyday citizen. Copland wanted people of future generations to listen to his music and get the feel of what it was like to live in the era when the music was written.

Materials

- ☐ "Hoe Down" from *Rodeo* (track 20–23 on *Copland Conducts Copland*, 2003, CD or other recording) and CD player (or cassette player or computer, depending on the recording)
- ☐ six 8½" x 11" sheets of cardstock
- ☐ permanent marker
- ☐ three drawings—two heads of horses, one beautiful girl (page 62)—to make puppets
- ☐ crayons, colored pencils, or colored markers
- ☐ three dowels or craft sticks
- ☐ tape or glue
- ☐ scissors
- ☐ one large piece of heavyweight fabric such as felt or denim, approximately 52" x 42" (or a large piece of cardboard or box for a puppet theater)
- ☐ student flow journals (see page 7)

Supplementary Materials

- ☐ orchestral score of *Rodeo* by Aaron Copland

Preparation

1. Use a large piece of fabric such as felt or denim to create a backdrop for the puppets. Follow the diagram below to make three sets of cuts in the fabric approximately 12 inches from the top and evenly spaced, left to right. These cuts should be 6 inches horizontally intersected by 6-inch vertical cuts. The fabric becomes your puppet stage; two students hold the fabric while other students standing behind it insert their puppets through the slots in the fabric. Another idea is to cut a square in a large piece of cardboard or a cardboard box.

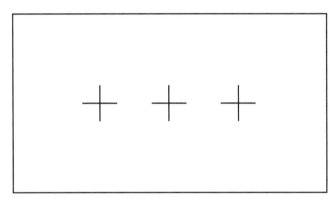

FABRIC PUPPET THEATRE EXAMPLE

2. Photocopy the drawings on page 62 of the two horses and the beautiful girl (or create your own drawings). Cut out the drawings, color them in (or have students do this), and attach them to a dowel or craft stick with tape or glue. Alternatively, you could create sock puppets or paper lunch-bag puppets, using markers to draw the faces and other features and yarn for hair.

3. Create six signs out of the cardstock, each with one of the following words or letters written on it with marker: INTRODUCTION, A, B, BRIDGE, A, and CODA. These signs indicate the form of "Hoe Down" in Copland's *Rodeo*.

 ## Getting Students Excited about the Topic

1. Start by asking what students know about rodeos and ballets, then share some information about both. For example:

   ❝*Have you ever been to a rodeo? What would you expect to see there? Usually spectators sit in bleachers and view cowboys as they demonstrate lassoing steers and riding bucking broncos or large Brahman bulls. If you went to a ballet, you would see dancers in costumes, making graceful and precise movements to music that conveys a story or theme.* **99**

2. Summarize the story of Aaron Copland's *Rodeo*, as in the following script:

66 *The famous dancer Agnes de Mille approached Aaron Copland about writing a musical ballet based on a rodeo in which a cowgirl tries to get the attention of one of the cowboys. Copland agreed, and in his ballet, the dancers are ranch hands, buckaroos, and women.*

In the first scene, the cowboys gather for the weekly rodeo. The awkward, tomboyish cowgirl tries to impress the head wrangler by riding a bucking bronco, but when she is thrown off, the others laugh at her. The cowboy she is trying to attract asks the rancher's daughter to attend the dance that night. Still dressed in her pants and shirt, the lonesome cowgirl watches from the sidelines as the couples swirl gaily on the dance floor. When no one offers to dance with her, she runs off the scene, then returns completely transformed, wearing a pretty dress with a bow in her hair. The guests gaze at her in amazement, realizing she can be as pretty as any of the other girls. Now the cowboys flock around her. Although the head wrangler offers to dance with her, she favors another cowboy—the only one who had shown some kindness to her before she had emerged from her cocoon. **99**

Guided Practice

1. Describe the aims of the lesson (see Measurable Learning Objectives) to ensure that students have the learning goals in mind and understand the purpose of the activities.

2. Have the class sing several simple nursery rhymes or folk tunes and discover which melodies are repeated and which melodies are contrasting. For example, you might sing "Old MacDonald Had a Farm":

Line 1: Old MacDonald had a farm, ee-i, ee-i, oh.
Line 2: And on this farm he had some pigs, ee-i, ee-i, oh.
Line 3: With an oink, oink here, and an oink, oink there,
      Here an oink, there an oink, everywhere an oink, oink.
Line 4: Old MacDonald had a farm, ee-i, ee-i, oh.

The first theme is called the "A" theme. The contrasting tune is called the "B" theme. When the first tune reappears, it is called "A." Thus in "Old MacDonald," Line 1 is A; line 2 is A; line 3 is B; and line 4 is A. The form for "Old MacDonald" is AABA.

3. Explain the arrangement of Copland's ballet into four dance episodes for orchestra: "Buckaroo Holiday," "Corral Nocturne," "Saturday Night Waltz," and "Hoe Down." The final movement, "Hoe Down," consists of a long introduction, the A theme, the B theme, a bridge, the A theme, and the coda, or tail. Explain to students that the bridge is music that connects two parts. The coda is like a tail added at the end for extra emphasis.

4. Play the recording of "Hoe Down" from *Rodeo.* Ask students to listen for the long introduction, the A theme, the B theme introduced by the trumpets, the bridge music, the returning A theme, and the coda. In the recording *Copland Conducts Copland,* the sections appear at the following places in the score and on a CD player counter:

   Beginning: Introduction (in two parts)
   A: Score marking 5; counter 0:40
   B: Score marking 12; counter 1:39
   Bridge: Score marking 17; counter 2:25
   A: Score marking 19; counter 2:51
   Coda: Score marking 22; counter 3:11
   (The entire movement is 3½ minutes long.)

5. Distribute the six signs to six students and have them stand facing the class at the front of the room, in the order of their signs' appearance in "Hoe Down."

6. Have two students stand holding the puppet backdrop so that three students can stand behind the material without being seen. Give a puppet to each of these three students. The beautiful girl puppet is in the middle.

7. Play "Hoe Down." As each section plays, the student holding the sign indicating that part of the form holds up his or her sign.

8. When the A theme appears, the student holding the first horse puppet (on the audience's left) puts the puppet through the opening in the fabric backdrop and dances the puppet in time to the music.

9. When the B theme plays, the first puppeteer pulls the horse out of the backdrop while the beautiful girl puppet comes out through the fabric backdrop and dances. No puppet dances during the bridge music; however the final horse puppet dances when the A theme reappears. When the coda appears, all puppets dance until the music stops.

10. Class members in the audience listen for the form and determine if the ones in the front of the room indicated the form at the right place in the music. Students in the front of the room and the puppeteers then change places with those seated until everyone has had a chance to participate.

Independent Practice

1. Have students sing or lead the class in singing a simple tune that indicates the A and B form of a song. For example, the form of "Rudolph the Red Nosed Reindeer" is AABA. Older students might bring to class or perform for the class a classical piece of music and identify its form.

2. Next, have students compose a simple song that follows the A and B form.

3. To connect the concept of form in music to other arts, have students bring to class pictures, or sketches they have drawn, illustrating the ABA symmetry in works of architecture, or have them choreograph and demonstrate dance movements with specific patterns that they can identify as the A, B, or C section.

Evaluation

Students will share with the class one of the following:

- A piece of music identifying the form—this could be a recording, music they perform, something they have composed, or a creative movement demonstration after which they identify the form.

- An original artwork that identifies the ABA form.

- A picture of a building that demonstrates the ABA or other form.

Reflection

- Ask students to share examples of how they reached the goals of this lesson. This could be an oral discussion or a writing assignment.

- Discuss with your students any aspects of flow that they experienced and add the information to the class flow chart (see page 5). Then ask students to make entries in their flow journals (see page 7). Young children could draw instead of write.

Extension

- Students could attend a program of classical music or a ballet and listen for the form of the music.

- Students could take a tour of the interesting architecture in their city and identify the patterns.

- Students could identify the form in pieces of music that they listen to and enjoy at home.

Chapter 9
Rules for Art and Life

Drawing Clowns

— Pat Hollingsworth —

Rules for Art and Life
– Drawing Clowns –

Drawing is a mode of expression, a method of communication, and way to reach the state of flow. Drawing is an engaging activity that is open ended and that differentiates for students' abilities. As a break from less imaginative schoolwork, drawing provides an opportunity to take risks and be creative that many students welcome. The activity in this chapter has a high rate of success with students. It is one in which nearly all your students will begin to see their potential as artists.

You can learn how to develop students' artistic abilities even if you do not consider yourself to be artistic. Drawing is a skill that can be learned; however, there are some interesting "rules" related to brain research that enable this to happen. This chapter explores these ideas while demonstrating ways to use drawing as a teaching tool.

Grades: K–8

Time Frame Options

30 to 40 minutes (younger children finish more quickly than older ones do)

Measurable Learning Objectives

Share these aims with students:

- Students will learn to be positive about their own artwork and that of others.
- Students will learn that they can draw.

Materials

- ☐ white construction paper or tagboard for each student
- ☐ crayons or oil pastels for each student
- ☐ Dr. Hollingsworth's Rules for Art and Life (page 74) for each student
- ☐ student flow journals (see page 7)

Supplementary Materials

For the extension (page 73), students will need watercolor sets, paint brushes, and water containers (large yogurt containers are the best because they do not tip over easily).

Preparation

1. Make copies of Dr. Hollingsworth's Rules for Art and Life (page 74) for students, unless the reading level is too high for your students. In that case, just have a copy in front of you and go over it with the class as described below.

CLOWN DRAWING

Active Learning: Increasing Flow in the Classroom, 2006 Crown House Publishing Company Ltd. www.crownhouse.co.uk

2. Set up each student with art supplies. Any type of paper will do, but tagboard or construction paper are good weights for this activity.

3. Review the clown-drawing illustration above.

 # Getting Students Excited about the Topic

1. Share the objectives of the lesson with students by first explaining that they can encourage their brains to work better by watching how they talk to themselves. For example, you might say,

> 66 *There are ways that you can help your brain do a better job. The best way to do that is to monitor what you say to your brain. Your brain works better when it is given encouraging words.* 99

2. Distribute Dr. Hollingsworth's Rules for Art and Life handout and go over each rule with students (or go over the rules without distributing them).

Guided Practice

During this part of the lesson, you will draw on the board and talk as the students are drawing at their desks. It is very important during this first lesson for everyone to feel successful. The drawing activity gives students a chance to use and practice the rules in a safe environment. Once students are used to following the rules, you can move to more challenging subjects.

Tell students that you will draw a clown picture on the board while they follow along on paper. Make sure they have their papers in the portrait orientation, not landscape, and remind them that the most important thing is that each of

I LOVE MAKING CLOWNS!

the drawings will be different. Talk them through the following steps while you draw on the board:

1. *Begin by making a large circle or oval that will be the clown's face.*

2. *Now draw a neck for the clown that has two sides, not just a stick neck, and make large shoulders that go off the page.*

3. *Let's now draw ears. Clowns might have large, small, or medium-size ears. You will decide which kind you want on your clown.*

4. *Now let's make hair for our clowns. You decide what kind of hair you want. You can make curly hair by going round and round. You may want to make wavy hair or straight hair. Make your decision and add the hair.*

5. *Next draw two eyes about in the middle of the face and a big round nose under the eyes.*

6. *Now decide what type of mouth you wish to draw for your clown. I am going to make a big smile on my clown.*

7. *Now I want you to draw a hat for your clown. It may be any kind of hat that you wish.*

8. Next draw a collar for your clown's shirt and then create a design pattern for the shirt and the hat. While you are doing that, I want to walk around and look at your artwork.

As you walk around to look at the artwork, give specific praise:

- I like the design you created on the clown's shirt.
- I like the way you drew the hair.
- I like the way each person's artwork is different.
- I like the way you kept on working even after you had created an "opportunity."

Independent Practice

Have students continue to work on their clowns:

❝ *Think of some other things that you would like to add to your clown picture. Would you want your clown to have balloons, a tiny car, or a bouquet of flowers? Keep thinking about what else you might add to your picture. Be sure to write your name in the bottom righthand corner of your picture.* **❞**

Closure

Close with enthusiasm:

❝ *You have created interesting and original pictures of clowns. Tomorrow you will be able to continue to work on your pictures. I liked how everyone followed the art rules, even when it was difficult to do so. I am glad that we were encouraging each other to keep our brains turned on by being positive with ourselves and with others.* **❞**

Evaluation

Use the Drawing and Attitude Rubric: Clowns (page 75) to evaluate each student's work and effort to follow the rules.

Reflection

- Ask students to share examples of how they reached the goals of this lesson. This could be an oral discussion or a writing assignment.

- Discuss with your students any aspects of flow they experienced and add the information to the class flow chart (see page 5). Ask students to make entries in their flow journals (see page 7). Young children could draw instead of write.

Extension

Have students add watercolors to their clown pictures.

1. Demonstrate and discuss how the oil-based crayons will resist being covered by the watercolors. Thus, students' drawings will still show up even when covered by the watercolors.

2. Explain that they should paint only one layer of watercolor on any one spot on their paintings. Once one area has been painted, students need to move on to find other white areas to paint. If a student tries to paint over one spot repeatedly, the paper will look as if it has been scrubbed.

3. Encourage students to use different colors and not to worry about getting an even shade across the picture. The beauty of watercolors is that each painted area will be slightly different. Watercolor painting is not like painting a wall. When painting a wall, one often wants one solid color. In a picture, one solid color can be visually boring.

Dr. Hollingsworth's Rules for Art and Life

1. Say only positive things about yourself and others. Put-downs cause you to be fearful and afraid of trying. To be creative and productive, you need to stay positive about yourself and others.

2. When you are having difficulties, say, "I created an opportunity." This will keep your attitude positive. It will give you time to see how you might use this opportunity.

3. If your art is not what you wanted, make it into something else. Do not scribble over or cross out your drawing. That is a good life skill because in life, things often happen that are not what you want. If life gives you a squashed tomato, make salsa!

4. Value your paper. Do not tear up, crumple, or throw away your paper. It has two sides. Pick one side and keep working on it. Life favors positive actions.

Active Learning: Increasing Flow in the Classroom, © 2006 Crown House Publishing Company Ltd. • www.crownhouse.co.uk

Drawing and Attitude Rubric: Clowns

Name: _____ Date: _____

	0	1	2	Points
Recognizable clown face	Not recognizable as a clown face	Somewhat recognizable as a clown face	Easily recognizable as a clown face	
Facial feature placement	Not correctly placed	Somewhat recognizably placed	Correctly placed	
Maintenance of a positive attitude	Did not have a positive attitude	Mostly maintained a positive attitude	Maintained a positive attitude	
			Total points:	

Scale:

6 = Excellent

5 = Very good

4 = Good

3 = Average

2 or below = Needs improvement

Chapter 10
Rules for Art and Life

Drawing Faces

— Pat Hollingsworth —

Rules for Art and Life

— Drawing Faces —

Grades: K–8

Time Frame Options

30 to 40 minutes (younger children finish more quickly than older ones do)

Measurable Learning Objectives

Share these aims with students:

- Students will learn to be positive about their own artwork and that of others.
- Students will be able to draw the faces of a man and a woman.

One of the first things babies learn to recognize is their own mother's face. One of the first things children draw is often a circle that later becomes a face. Why is it, then, that most people feel they cannot draw a straight line, much less a face? What happens that makes people feel so insecure about drawing? Drawing is a skill that can be learned, just like writing your name. Teachers need to create a safe atmosphere and provide some direct instruction to get students over their fear of drawing. Dr. Hollingsworth's Rules for Art and Life (page 74) help to create that safe atmosphere, giving students the opportunity to engage themselves in art and drawing. These are active learning activities that lead many people to the flow experience, while honing observation skills and encouraging the beginnings of art appreciation.

Materials

- ❏ white construction paper or tagboard for each student
- ❏ crayons or oil pastels for each student
- ❏ Dr. Hollingsworth's Rules for Art and Life (page 74) for each student
- ❏ student flow journals (see page 7)

Supplementary Materials

For the extension (page 81), students will need watercolor sets, paint brushes, and water containers (large yogurt containers are the best because they do not tip over easily).

Preparation

1. Set up each student with art supplies. Any type of paper will do, but tagboard or construction paper are good weights for this activity.

2. Review the face-drawing illustration on page 78.

Active Learning: Increasing Flow in the Classroom,
2006 Crown House Publishing Company Ltd.
www.crownhouse.co.uk

FACE DRAWING

Getting Students Excited about the Topic

Share the lesson objectives with students so that they understand and can relate to the goals of the drawing activity. Encourage students to approach drawing with a positive attitude by reminding them that drawing is a skill they can learn and by going over Dr. Hollingsworth's Rules for Art and Life (page 74). Compare drawing to learning to write your name to help students see that they don't need special talent to learn how to draw. For example:

> **"** *Drawing is a skill that everyone can learn, just like you learned to write your name. What is wonderful is that just like your handwriting, your drawing will be unlike anyone else's. Who can tell me one of the art rules? Who can tell why the rules are important? Yes, the main thing is that we all need our brains to stay turned on so that we can be creative and productive. We need our energy to be positive.* **"**

Guided Practice

Explain to students that you are going to draw the faces of a man and a woman on the board while they draw the same on their papers. Have them turn their papers to a landscape orientation so that they can get two faces beside each other on the paper. Remind them that the drawings should all look different when they are finished. Talk them through the following steps as you draw on the board.

HEADS

> **"** *Put your two hands flat on the paper in front of you. Now draw two ovals for the heads that are about that size. Each oval needs to be about the size of your hand when it is flat.* **"**

NECKS

"_Feel the size of your neck. Men generally have thicker necks than women do, so draw one of the necks thinner than the other. To make a neck, you need to draw two sides (not just a stick)._**"**

SHOULDERS

"_Feel the size and shape of your shoulders. Notice that you can see the top of your shoulder when you turn your head. Women generally have narrower shoulders than men have. Put narrower shoulders on the woman than on the man. Remember that the shoulders are much wider than the face._**"**

EARS

"_Feel where you ear starts and stops on your head, next to your face. It begins about even with the eyes and ends about even with the lips. Just draw a hint of ears. If you draw large ears, the face will look more like a clown._**"**

EYES

1. **"**_Look closely at the eyes of someone near you. Approximately where are the eyes in the face? The eyes of humans are about in the middle of the head. People often draw the eyes too high when drawing faces._**"**

2. **"**_Now look at the shape of the eyes, the color of the iris, the color of the pupil, and the reflection of light in the eyes._**"**

3. **"**_Draw two football-shaped eyes in the middle of each of the heads._**"**

4. **"**_In the middle of each football-shaped eye, put a large baseball shape. This circle should be large enough to fill the space from the top of the eye to the bottom._**"**

5. **"**_In the middle of the baseball shape, make a smaller black circle that is the pupil of the eye. The other part of the baseball shape is the iris, where we see the color of a person's eye. When you color the iris, leave one white spot in each eye to represent the light reflection. Now draw eyebrows and eyelashes, if you wish._**"**

NOSE

"_Just make an L for the nose. Later, as your drawing skills grow, you may wish to create more complicated noses._**"**

LIPS

"_Below the nose, draw a straight, horizontal line that will be the opening of the mouth. For the top lip, make a shape that looks like two low mountains. For the bottom lip, draw a shape that looks like a shallow bowl._**"**

Independent Practice

After students have the basic faces down on paper, encourage them to add details. Suggest possibilities to jump-start their imaginations:

- 66*Now decide what type of hair you want your people to have. Will it be curly, straight, or wavy? What kind of hair style will you select?*99

- 66*Choose the type of clothes, hat, or other head gear your people will wear. They might have crowns, baseball hats, helmets, straw hats, glasses, or something else. The choice is yours.*99

- 66*What kinds of things might be in the background? A castle, a playground, a city? The choice is yours.*99

Closure

Tell students that now that they have learned a way to draw faces, the more they observe people closely and practice drawing their faces, the better they will become at drawing them. Be sure to praise student attitudes:

66*I appreciate how positive you were during this difficult lesson and how you followed the art rules.*99

Evaluation

Use the Drawing and Attitude Rubric: Faces (page 82) for evaluating student work and attitudes.

Reflection

- Ask students to share examples of how they reached the goals of this lesson. This could be an oral discussion or a writing assignment.

- Discuss with your students any aspects of flow that they experienced and add the information to the class flow chart (see page 5). Then ask students to make entries in their flow journals (see page 7). Young children could draw instead of write.

Extension

- Continue with the process as often as possible to help students internalize both the drawing process and the positive attitude. The goal is for students to be able to draw faces independently.

- Students could color or paint the drawings they created. See the extension for drawing clowns (page 73) for tips on using watercolors.

- Have students draw pictures of animals you are studying in class. With each new drawing subject, do a walk-through drawing, with you on the board demonstrating while students follow along on their papers. This method gives you many opportunities for teaching. For example, when drawing a fish, ask students what fish have that people do not, how many fins fish have, and so on.

Drawing and Attitude Rubric: Faces

Name: _____ Date: _____

	0	1	2	Points
Recognizable human face	Not recognizable as a human face	Somewhat recognizable as a human face	Easily recognizable as a human face	
Facial feature placement	Not correctly placed	Somewhat recognizably placed	Correctly placed	
Maintenance of a positive attitude	Did not have a positive attitude	Mostly maintained a positive attitude	Maintained a positive attitude	
			Total points:	

Scale:

6 = Excellent

5 = Very good

4 = Good

3 = Average

2 or below = Needs improvement

Active Learning: Increasing Flow in the Classroom, © 2006 Crown House Publishing Company Ltd. • www.crownhouse.co.uk

Chapter 11

Exploring the World of Artists

Art in the Garden

— Donna Davilla —

Time Frame Options

- Pretrip introduction: 30 minutes
- Time in garden: 1½ to 2 hours
- Subsequent days: three to five 30- to 45-minute sessions

Measurable Learning Objectives

Share these aims with students:

- Students' drawings in the garden will be superior in detail and variety to those sketched prior to the field trip.
- Students will be able to identify the principles of design through the context of a garden.
- Students will demonstrate the application of the principles of design in creating a work of art.
- Students will be able to identify the art of Monet and O'Keeffe and compare their characteristic styles.
- Students' knowledge of plant names will increase.

Exploring the World of Artists

A s students return to the classroom in the late summer, their minds often linger on their experiences outdoors. A trip to a garden can be an enjoyable transition for students into a review of art vocabulary, an introduction to artists and design principles, practice in observation in both science and art, and a chance to express learning, connections, and inspiration in drawings and paintings. This type of learning asks students to recall their experiences and broaden their knowledge base for vocabulary, visual recognition, and application of their field trip experience. Active learning merges the visual, verbal, and kinesthetic in this lesson, offering opportunities also for science and art studies to merge.

Materials

- ☐ pencil and sketchbook for each student
- ☐ 3" x 5" index card for each student
- ☐ scissors
- ☐ set of nine colored flags or other cloths (a different colored set of nine for every two or three students)
- ☐ Principles of Design chart (page 90) for each student
- ☐ art prints or books of art featuring Claude Monet and Georgia O'Keeffe (see, for example, Castro 1985 and Nunhead 1994).
- ☐ Monet and O'Keeffe Venn Diagram (page 91) for each student
- ☐ Flower and Shrub Vocabulary chart (page 92) for each student
- ☐ student flow journals (see page 7)

Preparation

1. Arrange a field trip to a local garden. This can be a neighbor's garden near the school, a commercial garden, or a botanical garden. Try to arrange for the chief gardener to take you and your students on a walking tour. Be sure you get permission to have students leaving their colored flags or cloth in different places around the garden (temporarily).

2. Arrange the field trip with your school and parents, including permission slips, lunch, transportation, and so forth as you are required to do.

3. Photocopy all handouts: Principles of Design chart (page 90); Monet and O'Keeffe Venn Diagram (page 91); and Flower and Shrub Vocabulary chart (page 92).

4. Create a viewfinder for each student by cutting a small square (about 1 ½") in the center of each index card.

5. Gather Monet and O'Keeffe prints or books for the classroom and for taking with you on the field trip.

 # Getting Students Excited about the Topic

1. Engage students by reminding them of the summer and promising a taste of the outdoors:

   > **“**Do you remember a wonderful time that you had outdoors this summer? You might have been playing ball, hiking, or just walking about your neighborhood. Today we are going to be outdoors in a garden to sketch and to learn more about the principles of design.**”**

2. Share the aims of the lesson with students, as described in the Measurable Learning Objectives section, so that they understand and relate to what they will achieve. Summarize the four main tasks students will accomplish on the field trip:

   - In small groups, they will identify each principle of design on the chart (page 90) as they find it in the garden.

   - Students will think about the differences between the artistic styles of Claude Monet and Georgia O'Keeffe, as discussed in Guided Practice in the Classroom (page 86), before they leave for the field trip.

   - Students will make sketches while in the garden, looking carefully at the details of plants and especially the flowers as they draw. Later, they will create paintings based on the principles of design they identify in the garden.

OBSERVING NATURE

- Students will need to pay attention to the names of plants and try to expand their knowledge of them.

Guided Practice in the Classroom

1. As students arrive in the classroom on the day of the field trip, ask each of them to make quick sketches of flowers during the first five minutes.

2. After the sketches are completed, engage students in a discussion of gardens they have seen:

   ❝What was special about that garden? Where is it located? Who introduced you to it?**❞**

3. Next have students write as many names of flowers or other fauna as they can recall in the Flower and Shrub Vocabulary chart (page 92).

4. Lead a discussion about French artist Claude Monet. Explain how he created his own garden, which inspired his paintings. Show examples. Discuss art vocabulary of foreground, middle ground, and background. Have students practice pointing out each through art slides or prints.

5. Discuss the differences between Monet's work and O'Keeffe's. Show prints or examples from books and lead students to notice that Monet often painted landscapes and O'Keeffe often painted extreme closeups, particularly of flowers.

6. Have students start working on the Monet and O'Keeffe Venn Diagram (page 91).

7. Before leaving for the garden, remind students of the four main tasks ahead of them (pages 85–86).

Guided Practice in the Garden

1. If you've arranged for a walking toured by the chief gardener, ask him or her to explain special features of the garden. Emphasize some of the scientific names of flowers.

2. After the tour, bring students back together and hand out the Principles of Design chart (page 90).

3. Go over these principles, elaborating on their meaning and showing visual clues through examples. Explain that the list of these principles may vary depending upon which art reference book is used. The principles describe how the elements of art are used and organized.

Independent Practice with Principles of Design

1. Give each student a sketchbook, a pencil, and a viewfinder.

2. Ask students to divide into teams of two or three students. Each team will work together in the garden to find examples of the principles of design on the chart. Each team will be identified by the color of their own set of colored flags, one flag for each principle of design on the chart. Set a time for students to reassemble at an easy-to-find location in the garden (make sure each team has at least one member with a watch).

3. Each team then walks around the garden, finding examples of each of the principles on the list. Encourage students to use the viewfinder to help focus their view.

4. When they find a principle, the students place their colored flag to mark the spot and then note on the chart where they found the principle.

5. At the end of the set time, have students reassemble.

6. Going down the principles list, ask each team to describe for the group its example of that principle—how that principle is demonstrated in the flowers, bushes, other plants, or other objects in the garden. Students retrieve their flags as the class walks from example to example.

7. After this exercise, lead a brief discussion on American artist Georgia O'Keeffe. Using art prints, show the attention to details and close up views that O'Keeffe used in her flower paintings.

8. Next lead the students in a discussion comparing the works of Monet and O'Keeffe. Remind them that they will complete their Monet and O'Keeffe Venn Diagrams when back at school.

Independent Practice with Drawing

1. Students then go into the garden and select a view to draw in detail. They can use either a Monet-inspired landscape approach or an O'Keeffe-inspired closeup view.

2. In the Flower and Shrub Vocabulary chart, students write the names of flowers and other plants in the garden and compare them to their previous knowledge.

3. Alert students ten minutes before it's time to leave the garden. This will give them a chance to finish particular details of their artwork. When they gather prior to leaving, remind them that they were successful in identifying the principles of design and that the lesson will continue with their creation of paintings based on their drawings in the garden.

Independent Practice in the Classroom

1. Students return to the classroom and compare their preliminary sketches with the ones completed on location.

2. Have students write briefly about how their drawings changed.

3. During subsequent art classes, students will create paintings based on their direct observational drawings.

Evaluation

■ Have students complete and turn in their Principles of Design sheet, Venn diagram, and Flower and Shrub Vocabulary sheet.

■ A class discussion of what was learned through this lesson will cover the following:

> **"** *How do the before and after drawings compare? Was there any new learning about details found in nature?* **"**

> **"** *Are you able to use and describe the principles of design in your paintings?* **"**

> **"** *Do you have a larger vocabulary? If so, what new words did you learn?* **"**

> **"** *What did you learn about the principles of design in a garden?* **"**

Reflection

■ Ask students to share examples of how they reached the goals of this lesson. This could be an oral discussion or a writing assignment.

■ Discuss with your students any aspects of flow that they experienced and add the information to the class flow chart (see page 5). Then ask students to make entries in their flow journals (see page 7).

Extension

■ Extended learning could include math. In the garden, can students find even numbers in nature? Are multiples used in garden designs?

■ Have students work together to create their own garden landscape designs. How will they organize it and what will be included? This can help build team decision-making. Provide books of landscape architecture designs as inspiration, or ask a landscape architect to bring designs to share and discuss with the class.

Principles of Design

Name: _____ Date: _____

Design Principle	Principle Found	Where?
Rhythm: repetition, sequence, alternation, pattern, movement		
Balance: formal, informal		
Emphasis: central focus, one element stressed		
Contrast: emphasis of strong differences in the art elements		
Unity: feeling of completeness or wholeness		
Radiation: coming out from a center		
Transition: gradual change in color or size		
Variety: slight changes or differences		
Proportion: adjustment of size; relationship of one part to another and to the whole		

Monet and O'Keeffe Venn Diagram

Name: _____ Date: _____

Use any of the phrases in the list or add your own.

Claude Monet   **Georgia O'Keeffe**

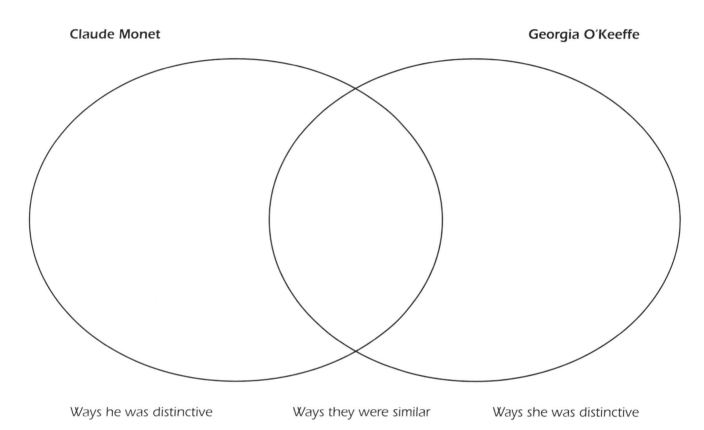

Ways he was distinctive   Ways they were similar   Ways she was distinctive

Impressionistic landscapes
American artist
Concern with detail
Magnified flowers
French artist
Individualistic styles
Closeup views
Water gardens
Painted nature

Flower and Shrub Vocabulary

Name: _____ Date: _____

Before the trip

Make a list of all the flowers and shrubs you can.

During or after the trip

Make a list of all the flowers and shrubs you see (or saw) in the garden.

Chapter 12

The History of Architecture

From Egyptian to Modern

— Alicia Parent —

Time Frame Options

- One step a week for 10 weeks
- Two steps a day for a week
- One step a day for two weeks
- One step every two weeks for 20 weeks

Measurable Learning Objectives

Share these aims with students:

- Students will be able to identify characteristics of architecture styles from the various time periods.
- Students will understand the cultural values that influenced various styles of Western architecture.
- Students will be able to draw a chronological history of Western architecture.
- Students will be able to compare and contrast various architectural styles.

The History of Architecture

This multiday unit teaches an ongoing chant with accompanying movements that represent various architectural styles. The chant represents a sequence of the architecture of Western civilization. By being physically involved in bringing historical elements to life, students are more likely to remember the historical features of the timeline. Thus the chant, which becomes embedded in memory, provides a symbol, or advance organizer, for more in-depth learning.

Elementary and middle school students are able to learn advanced concepts when they approach them in an active way. When students become physically involved in the study of architecture, they retain information and gain understanding of key concepts from this discipline. This basic architectural knowledge creates a foundation for and recognition of the values and ideals of a culture as reflected in the art and architecture of that culture. This unit focuses on basic architectural examples from pre-eminent historical time periods, organized in 10 steps.

Materials

- ☐ folder for each student with 20 sheets of blank paper and architectural handouts: Architecture Chant (page 95), History of Architecture (page 120), 10 architectural examples (drawings throughout this chapter), and Roman Gods and Goddesses (page 117)

- ☐ pencils, colored pencils, pens, markers

- ☐ poster-size enlargements of the 10 architectural examples (pages 99, 103, 107, 111, 114)

- ☐ student flow journals (see page 7)

Architecture Chant

E-e-gyptian

1. mural 2. pyramid

Greek

Parthenon pediment
(classical)

Roman

Pantheon dome
(classical)

Romanesque

tall, thick arch

Gothic

Gothic spire

Renaissance
(say twice)

1. classical pediment
2. classical dome

Baroque
(say 3 times)

twisted
columns

Neoclassical
(say twice)

1. classical pediment
2. classical dome

Romantic

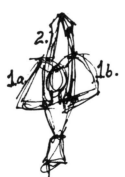

1. dramatic sweep of each
   hand to forehead
2. Gothic spire

Modern
(say twice)

cantilevered arms
like Egyptian mural

From SAILS *Teacher's Resource Book,* © 2000, reprinted by permission of University School at the University of Tulsa,
www.uschool.utulsa.edu.

Supplementary Materials

☐ Additional illustrations and photo examples of architecture from each time period (See the photos available in the SAILS curriculum materials, available at www.uschool.utulsa.edu.)

☐ *Art of the Western World* (Cole and Gealt 1989) or another comprehensive book about Western art and architecture.

Preparation

1. Review this entire unit before you begin, adapting the scripts and steps to fit the details you wish to teach and the wording appropriate for your particular students. If necessary, review information about the various architectural styles (such as in *Art of the Western World*) so that you are prepared to answer questions and feel comfortable with the information.

2. Gather the necessary materials and make all photocopies, creating a folder for each student as described above and enlarging the 10 architectural examples to poster size (or 11" x 17").

3. Clear enough space in your classroom for groups of five to ten students to move freely.

4. Plan ahead for the Architecture in Your City field trip (see page 118) by scouting out the route first so that the class sees as many different architectural elements as possible. Bring a copy of the History of Architecture handout (page 120) to fill out so that you have an idea of how many and which elements students are likely to find on the trip. Prepare permission letters for parents and take care of any administrative requirements your school has for taking field trips, especially if you will need a bus for the trip.

Getting Students Excited about the Topic

1. Before starting the first step in this unit, ask students questions that start them thinking about architecture in their lives. For example:

   ■ What is the most famous building that you know?
   ■ What kinds of buildings would you like to see?
   ■ What is the oldest building that you know?

2. After discussing student answers to these questions, connect the discussion to the upcoming unit. For example:

   “ *The buildings we have just discussed have something in common. Many are great pieces of architecture, and they all represent the historical time period in which they were built.* **”**

3. Introduce the objectives of the unit by explaining the connection between architecture and the cultural needs and values of the people who created it in a given time period. For example:

> 66 *Throughout history people have created art and architecture that reflected their own needs and ideals. Sometimes they looked back in time and adapted styles they appreciated from other years, but they always made it their own. They created new elements based on their needs and desires.* 99

4. Provide an example to illustrate how people adapt architecture to fit their needs and desires, then use this example to introduce the objective of looking at architectural development as a way to understand people of various time periods. For example, you might show the Gothic cathedral drawing (page 107) to the class and explain:

> 66 *Before the huge Gothic cathedrals could be created, the builders and designers had to discover a way to keep the tall, thin walls and stained glass windows from falling down. Their answer was an external support system called a flying buttress. Our study of architecture will show us how it has developed over the years. We can also learn about the people who created it.* 99

Step 1: Egyptian

Guided Practice

1. Explain to students that they will be learning chants and movements to help them learn about architectural styles. For example:

> 66 *Today we are going to begin learning a chant with movements that will be the foundation of the architecture unit we are going to study. Once you have learned the chants and the movements that go with it for each architectural period, you will have an overview of the history of Western architecture.* 99

2. Have students turn to the Architecture Chant page in their folders (on page 95 of this book). Explain that they are going to imitate the movement in the first figure (E-e-gyptian) while saying "E-e-gyptian" in unison. For example:

“*First, you will stand like an Egyptian person on a tomb painting, and then make a pyramid shape with your arms, as shown on the handout. Stand up and try that movement while we say 'E-e-gyptian' together. For each time period we study, we will use our bodies to create the shape of a building from that period. Today, we are creating the shape of a pyramid.*”

3. Have students look at the picture of a pyramid in their folders (page 99 of this book). Provide details about ancient Egyptian culture that are relevant to this architecture, such as belief in the afterlife and the value of permanence and stability. Add any other details about the connection between ancient Egyptian culture and architecture that you wish students to learn or that you think they will find engaging. For example, you might say:

“*The Egyptians believed in and valued the afterlife, so they created the pyramids as burial chambers to help them cross over into the eternal afterlife. The main points to remember are that the Egyptians valued permanence, stability, and the afterlife. Their architecture reflects those values in the building of the pyramids. A pyramid is a very stable shape. It is like a mountain created by humans. It is not easily blown away or destroyed.*

“*The pharaohs were entombed in the pyramids with everything they thought they would need in the afterlife. They expected the afterlife to be just like Egyptian life except that it would be for eternity. So they stocked their pyramids with an abundance of food, clothing, jewelry, games, furniture, and sometimes even chariots.*”

Independent Practice

1. Divide the students into groups of five or six. Explain that each group is to use four people to create a pyramid using their bodies. One or two students will be inside the pyramid, planning the pharaoh's burial chamber. As a group, students should discuss and imagine how the walls of the chamber would look and what items the pharaoh would want in the chamber.

2. Next have students each draw on a blank page in their folders what they imagine the pyramid and chamber to look like.

3. While they are drawing, write these keywords on the board:
Egyptians = Afterlife = Pyramids. Have students also make drawings

EGYPTIAN

GREEK

From SAILS *Teacher's Resource Book,* © 2000, reprinted by permission of University School at the University of Tulsa, www.uschool.utulsa.edu.

on another blank page in their folders that represent these keywords for Egyptian architecture, and have them write the keywords at the bottom of their Egyptian drawings.

Step 2: Greek

Guided Practice

1. Have students turn to the Architecture Chant page in their folders (page 95 in this book) and look at the second movement, noticing that the arms form a triangle.

2. Ask students what part of the Greek building this triangle represents (a pediment, which is a characteristic feature of classical Greek architecture). Point out that the most famous Greek temple is the Parthenon in Athens, Greece. The eight columns on each end of the building support the pediment.

3. Explain that students will imitate the movement in the second figure on the Architecture Chant page while saying the word "Greek," as well as the first figure they learned during their study of Egypt, while saying "E-e-gyptian":

   66 *Today you will use your arms to create the triangular shape of the Parthenon pediment. Now stand up and do the first two movements of the chant while we say 'E-e-egyptian' and 'Greek' together.* **99**

4. Next, discuss the parallels between classical Greek architecture and the society it reflects, using any of numerous details on which you want students to focus. For example:

   66 *Let's again look at the drawing of the Parthenon. The Greeks highly valued balance and order. They believed that people should live orderly, balanced lives in which both the mind and body were important. The creators of the Parthenon wanted those values to be evident in their temple.*

   66 *The Parthenon was dedicated to the goddess of wisdom, Athena, whose symbol is the owl. When the Athenians came to worship, they stood outdoors and looked at the Parthenon and at the 40-foot-tall*

SKETCHING BUILDINGS

statue of Athena that was beside the Parthenon. Athena wore a helmet, had a huge shield, and held a long spear.

❝ *The Parthenon was built on the acropolis, a tall hill in Athens. In times of war, the acropolis was used as a place from which to defend the city. The famous general Pericles was the leader who had the Parthenon built. His leadership was so outstanding that the time is called 'The Golden Age of Pericles.' Where do you see simplicity, symmetry, and balance in the Parthenon? The main points to remember are that the Greeks valued a balanced life, and their architecture reflects that in the Parthenon.* **❞**

Independent Practice

1. Divide students into groups of five or six and have them create the Parthenon with their bodies. One person will be Athena, one will be General Pericles, and the others will be the Parthenon.

2. As a group, students should talk about the importance of balance, harmony, and order in the world. Each group will have a chance to share their creation of the Parthenon and their ideas about Greek values.

3. Next have students draw in their folders their own pictures of the Parthenon, the acropolis, Athena, and Pericles. While they are drawing, write the keywords for the ancient Greeks on the board (Greeks = Balance = Parthenon) and ask students to include them at the bottoms of their drawings.

Step 3: Roman

Guided Practice

1. Have students turn to the Architecture Chant page in their folders (page 95 in this book) and look at the third movement.

2. Ask them what part of the Roman Pantheon the shape represents (the dome). Note that the Romans placed the dome on top of a pediment with columns like the classical Greek architecture in the Parthenon.

3. Now students stand up and do the first three movements of the chant while saying "E-e-egyptian," "Greek," and "Roman."

4. Have students look at the picture of the Pantheon (page 103 of this book) while you describe the key characteristics of Roman society and how these are reflected in the architecture. For example:

> 66 *The Romans had a powerful civilization with advanced technology, and they liked to build things. They valued the ideals and accomplishments of the Greeks, so they borrowed the Parthenon style of architecture and added a dome, which took great technological skill. Each concentric circle of the dome was made with lighter and lighter material so that it would support itself. The Pantheon was a temple built to honor all the gods. Statues of these gods and goddesses were around the inside circumference of the building in little recessed areas called niches. The height of the dome is 142 feet and the diameter of the inside is also 142 feet. There is a 30-foot-wide hole in the dome called the oculus. Sunlight would stream through the oculus and highlight different gods and goddesses at different times of day. In order to distinguish the Parthenon and Pantheon in my mind, I remember that a pan is round, which reminds me of the word 'Pantheon.'* 99

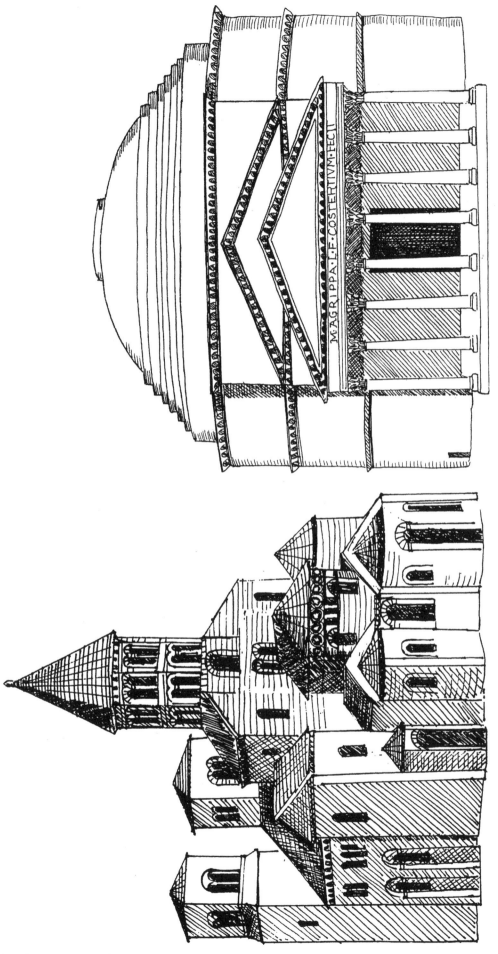

ROMAN

ROMANESQUE

Independent Practice

1. Divide students into groups of six or seven and have them review the sheet called "Roman Gods and Goddesses" (page 117). Each person selects a different god or goddess to represent as the group creates the inside of the Pantheon with their bodies.

   *Stand in a circle facing each other as if you were a god or goddess inside the Pantheon. One person in the center of the group, just under the oculus, will represent the sun. As the person representing the sun points to you, make actions that describe which god or goddess you are. For example, if you are Mars, you might make fighting actions; if you are Mercury, you might run in place. Remember, you must stay within your niche.***

2. Next have students draw pictures in their folders of the Pantheon and any gods or goddesses they wish. As they draw, write the keywords on the board: Roman = Power = Pantheon. Have students write these under their drawings.

Step 4: Romanesque

Guided Practice

1. Have students turn to the Architecture Chant page in their folders (page 95 in this book) and look at the fourth movement, which resembles the dome shape for the Roman Pantheon but is taller. Students will use a deeper voice for this part of the chant than they used with the Roman. Point out that "Romanesque" means "like the Roman" but that Roman-esque buildings were fortresses to keep out the barbarians.

2. Have students stand up and do the first four movements of the chant while you all say "E-e-egyptian," "Greek," "Roman," and "Romanesque" (in a deep voice).

POETS AND ARTISTS AT SCHOOL

3. Have students look at pictures of Romanesque architecture, such as the one on page 103 in this book. Note that the rounded style of the Roman arch was used frequently for monasteries and castles. Provide additional background details of your choosing, such as the following:

> ❝ When the Roman Empire became weak and fell, hoards of invaders attacked, which ushered in a period that is called by different names: Middle Ages, Dark Ages, or the Medieval period. The Middle Ages, which lasted about 1,000 years, was a difficult time when there was little law and order. Buildings had to have thick walls and small windows to withstand the vicious attacks that occurred. Castles were frequently built as fortresses in the Middle Ages. They also had thick walls, few doors, and tiny windows.

> ❝ The Romanesque buildings of the Middle Ages reflect the needs of the people for safety and some measure of security. People did not expect to live long, so they put their hope and faith in their religion. Their values are revealed in the architecture of castles and cathedrals. ❞

Independent Practice

1. Divide students into groups of six or seven students to create a Romanesque building or castle with their bodies.

   > "*Four of you create the building while others are the occupants of the building. If your building is a castle, someone will need to be king. If your building is a monastery, some of you will be the monks. Perhaps you might sing a Gregorian chant. Each group will share their building and its occupants with the whole class.*"

2. Next have students draw in their folders pictures of Romanesque buildings and their occupants. Write keywords on the board for them to place under their drawings: Romanesque = Middle Ages = Defense and Religion = Castles and Churches.

 Step 5: Gothic

Guided Practice

1. Have students turn to the Architecture Chant page in their folders (page 95 in this book) and look at the fifth movement—arms straight up like a church spire or steeple. Explain that near the end of the Middle Ages, life was becoming more stable, cities were being formed, and there were fewer invasions. This was the time when Gothic cathedrals were first created. They had tall spires, thin walls, huge stained glass windows, and flying buttresses to support all the weight. The Gothic cathedrals often used pointed arches rather than the round Romanesque or Roman arches.

2. When students do the spire movement, they will say "Gothic" by making their voices go up high, like a spire, on the ending part of the word:

   > "*Now stand up and do the first five movements of the chant while we say 'E-e-egyptian,' 'Greek,' 'Roman,' 'Romanesque (deep voice),' 'Gothic (high voice).'*"

GOTHIC

RENAISSANCE

GEORGE AND BEN VISIT THE CLASSROOM

3. Explain details about the period, or focus in this instance on the person primarily responsible for the changes in architecture Gothic style heralded. You might focus on Abbot Suger, for example:

> ❝ *Abbot Suger, from France, first conceived of the idea to create a different kind of cathedral. He wanted sunlight to pour into the churches like the light of God. He imagined huge round windows in beautiful colors of glass that are now often called 'rose windows.' He imagined strong arched arms of concrete to support the thin walls and large windows. Abbot Suger also wanted to use pointed arches, gargoyles, and beautiful designs on the churches.* ❞

Independent Practice

1. Divide students into groups of nine or ten to create a Gothic cathedral using their bodies (two students as stained glass windows; two as spires; four as flying buttresses; one as Abbot Suger; and one as a gargoyle to protect the cathedral). As they are building, students should talk about what it will look like when finished.

2. Then students draw a Gothic cathedral in their folders. As they draw, write the keywords on the board for them to put under their drawings: Gothic = Middle Ages = Looking to God = Soaring Spires and Flying Buttresses.

 Step 6: Renaissance

Note: Chapter 13, "Renaissance and Baroque Art" is a good resource to use in conjunction with this lesson.

Guided Practice

1. Have students turn to the Architecture Chant page in their folders (page 95 in this book) and look at the sixth movement—arms first making a triangle pediment shape like the Parthenon, and then making the dome shape like the Roman Pantheon. People were so tired of the Middle Ages, they wanted something to remind them of past glories and greatness. "Renaissance" means rebirth of the ideals of the classical Greeks and Romans.

2. Now have students stand up and do the first six movements of the chant while you all say "E-e-egyptian," "Greek," "Roman," "Romanesque" (deep voice), "Gothic" (high voice), "Ren-ai-ssance, Ren-ai-ssance."

3. Describe characteristic of the period and the architectural parallels you wish to highlight. For example:

> 66 *The Renaissance was a time for the revival of interest in education and learning. In this period from about AD 1350 to 1600, people continued their interest in religion, but they were also interested in mythology, arms and armor, classical architecture and sculpture, scientific experiments, and exploration and conquests of other lands. This is the time of the voyages of Columbus and many others.*

> 66 *The dome for the Florence cathedral was created by Brunelleschi. It was a great technological feat. No one had created such a dome before. In addition to domes, Renaissance buildings used round Roman arches and Greek-style pediments. The architects did not try to compete with Gothic cathedrals in terms of size; the buildings were closer to human proportions.* 99

Independent Practice

1. Divide students into groups of six or seven to use their bodies to create a Renaissance building with a dome:

   “Some of you will create the dome while others are pediments and Roman arches. Others of you will be Renaissance artists, architects, or sculptors. As the building is being created, discuss the values of the period, such as interest in biblical and mythological subjects, interest in Greek and Roman art and architecture, and interest in science and explorations. **”**

2. Then have students draw Renaissance buildings and artwork while you write the keywords on the board for them to put under their drawings: Renaissance = Rebirth of Classical Ideals = Tall Domes

Step 7: Baroque

Guided Practice

1. Have students turn to the Architecture Chant page in their folders (page 95 in this book) and look at the seventh movement—arms making a triangle pediment shape combined with a twisting motion.

2. Explain that the twisting movement symbolizes the ornate and swirling Baroque era, then have students stand up and do the first seven movements of the chant while they say “E-e-egyptian,” “Greek,” “Roman,” “Romanesque” (deep voice), “Gothic” (high voice), “Ren-ai-ssance, Ren-ai-ssance,” “Ba-roque, Ba-roque, Ba-roque.”

3. Describe details of the Baroque era and architecture. You might say,

   “The Baroque era was a time of dramatic energy, kingly power, and ornate and embellished surfaces. Baroque architects took the basic Renaissance building and embellished it with oval windows, twisted columns, curved and swirling frames, and heavily decorated surfaces, many of them with goldleaf. **”**

BAROQUE

NEOCLASSICAL

Independent Practice

1. Divide students into groups of six or seven to create an ornate Baroque palace using their bodies. At least two people will need to be twisted columns. Two people will need to be the king and queen who are commissioning the elaborate building. Students should talk about all the things the building needs so that it is grander than the "old-fashioned and out-dated" Renaissance buildings. Each group will share their building ideas with the whole group.

2. Then students draw pictures of elaborate Baroque palaces and buildings, while you write the the keywords on the board for them to put under their pictures: Baroque = Dramatic = Ornamental Dome and Twisted Columns.

 Step 8: Neoclassical

Guided Practice

1. Have students turn to the Architecture Chant page in their folders (page 95 in this book) and look at the eighth movement, an exact repeat of the Renaissance movement because the neoclassical period was a repeat. The era looked back to the Renaissance and to classical Greek and Roman arts, architecture, and ideals.

2. Have students stand up and do the first eight movements of the chant while they say "E-e-egyptian," "Greek," "Roman," "Romanesque" (deep voice), "Gothic" (high voice) "Ren-ai-ssance, Ren-ai-ssance," "Ba-roque, Ba-roque, Ba-roque," "neo-classical, neo-classical."

3. Have students look at the images of the Pantheon (page 103) and of Monticello (page 111). Can they see why this architecture is called "neo" or new classical? You might note that our forefathers looked back to the classical period when they fashioned this architecture and our government. Ask students what kinds of ideals Washington and Jefferson wanted our country to have. Remind them that the neoclassical period was a swing back from the overindulgent Baroque to the simple classical era.

Independent Practice

1. Divide students into groups of four or five to create neoclassical buildings using their bodies:

   ❝ *You might select Monticello, the White House, the United States Capitol Building, or other federal office buildings. What buildings in our city are in the neoclassical style? As your group creates a neoclassical building, talk about the ideals that Jefferson and Washington wanted for our country. Be ready to share your building and ideas with the class in a few minutes.* **❞**

2. Students then draw neoclassical buildings and events in their folders. Have them also create a drawing that illustrates how the Greek and the Roman architecture were similar to the neoclassical. Write the keywords on the board for students to put under their drawings: Neoclassical = Looking Back to Classical = Monticello and White House.

 Step 9: Romantic

Guided Practice

1. Have students turn to the Architecture Chant page in their folders (page 95 in this book) and look at the ninth movement, which has three parts: each hand alternately sweeps dramatically across the forehead and ends with both arms straight overhead like a spire or steeple. The romantics looked to the Middle Ages for inspiration, often seeing the past in a dreamy, idealized way.

2. Next students stand up and do the first nine movements of the chant: "E-e-egyptian," "Greek," "Roman," "Romanesque" (deep voice), "Gothic" (high voice), "Ren-ai-ssance, Ren-ai-ssance," "Ba-roque, Ba-roque, Baroque," "neo-classical, neo-classical," "ro-man-tic" (draw out the word).

3. Have students look at the pictures of the romantic period, such as the image on page 114 of this book. Explain the characteristics of the period that are reflected in the architecture, such as by focusing on comparisons to other eras:

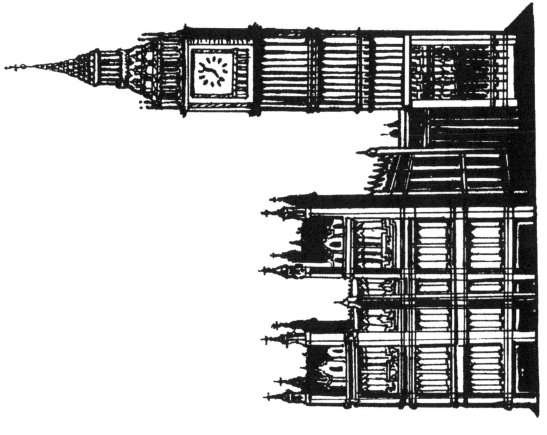

ROMANTIC

MODERN

"Just as neoclassical architecture was looking back, so was the romantic. Which period does this resemble? Yes, the romantics looked back to the medieval times for inspiration in an idealistic way. For example, in the Middle Ages, castles were cold, dark fortresses. In the romantic period, they were elaborate pleasure palaces much like a palace in a Disney movie. The romantics idealized nature and war, loved exotic lands and animals, and were dramatic, similar to the values in the Baroque era."

Independent Practice

1. Divide students into groups of five or six to create a romantic palace using their bodies. Students should talk about what they would want in this elaborate pleasure palace.

2. Then students draw a picture of romantic architecture and compare it to the medieval while you write the keywords on the board for them to put under their drawings: Romantic = Looking Back to Medieval = Palaces and Exotic Lands.

 Step 10: Modern

Guided Practice

1. Have students turn to the Architecture Chant page in their folders. Explain that today they are going to imitate the movement in the tenth figure (Modern) while saying "modern, modern" in unison. Have them practice this chant and movement together.

2. Point out that the tenth movement looks like the movement for Egyptian architecture, and that this represents how modern architecture borrows from all time periods. For example:

"In modern times, people have borrowed from all the time periods. Modern architecture often has cantilevered features, where a structure extends well beyond its support. The tenth movement is both a tribute to all past architecture and to the cantilevered features of modern architecture."

3. Have students look at the modern architecture illustration in their folders (on page 114 of this book). You might also pass around or display other modern architectural examples, such as photos or illustrations from a book or the Internet. Provide details about modern architecture, such as by giving an example of a modern architect.

> **“***Frank Lloyd Wright is perhaps the most well known architect of the twentieth century. His work used cantilevering as well as many other inventive features.***”**

4. Next, everyone stands up to do all 10 movements of the chant:

> **“***'E-e-gyptian,' 'Greek,' 'Roman,' 'Romanesque' (deep voice), 'Gothic' (high voice), 'Ren-ai-ssance, Ren-ai-ssance,' 'Ba-roque, Ba-roque, Ba-roque,' 'neo-classical, neo-classical,' 'ro-man-tic' (draw out the word), 'modern, modern.' Now clap.***”**

Independent Practice

1. Divide students into groups of six or seven and have them create a modern building with their bodies. Two of them will be architects who are deciding what type of building to create.

2. Next have students draw a modern building on a blank page in their folders.

3. As they draw, write these keywords on the board: Modern = Borrowing from All Eras = Frank Lloyd Wright. Have them illustrate these keywords on another blank page, writing the keywords under their drawings.

Culminating Projects

- **Chronology Chant Game:** Give 10 students each one of the architectural example posters you created. Explain that each poster represents a different period of architecture. Have these students stand so that their posters are in the correct chronological order. The rest of the class then does the chant and movements for each style.

  Next, have the students give their posters to someone who has not had one. As soon as the new group is in correct chronological order, the rest of the students will repeat the chants and movements.

Roman Gods and Goddesses

Jupiter—ruler of the gods

Juno—Jupiter's wife

Ceres—goddess of growing things

Cupid—god of love

Diana—goddess of hunting

Mars—god of war

Mercury—messenger of gods

Minerva—goddess of crafts, war, and wisdom

Neptune—god of the sea

Pluto—god of the underworld

Somnus—god of sleep

Venus—goddess of love

Vesta—goddess of the hearth

Vulcan—blacksmith of the gods

- **Comparison Group Presentations:** Once the chant and the time period reviews are familiar, divide the students into five groups to discuss the patterns and repetitions that are found in architecture. Each group has a different assignment:

  Compare the Parthenon with the Pantheon
  Compare Romanesque with Gothic architecture
  Compare Baroque with neoclassical architecture
  Compare medieval with romantic architecture
  Compare Renaissance with classical Greek and Roman architecture

  Each group makes a list of similarities and differences and creates a class presentation that includes all group members.

- **Architecture in Your City:** As a class take a walking tour or bus tour of your neighborhood or city. Have each student bring the History of Architecture handout (page 120). Encourage each student to make a notation each time he or she sees a building with one of the architectural elements listed on the handout. When you return to class, discuss the examples found and not found.

Closure

End the unit by summarizing the learning. For example:

❝ *You have learned about the history of architecture from ancient Egypt to modern times and that there are many examples of various time periods in our community today. You have learned that the values and ideas of a culture influence its architecture.* **❞**

Evaluation

- Evaluate students' knowledge by having them fill out the History of Architecture (page 120), which requires drawing each of the architectural styles studied.

- Use the Presentations Rubric (page 127) to evaluate the various presentations that student groups make.

Reflection

- Ask students to share examples of how they reached the goals of this lesson. This could be an oral discussion or a writing assignment.

- Discuss with your students any aspects of flow that they experienced and add the information to the class flow chart (see page 5). Then ask students to make entries in their flow journals (see page 7).

Extension

- Ask students to create a mnemonic to remember the order of the time periods. (For example: **E**very **g**irl **r**uns **r**apidly, **g**oing **r**ighteously **b**eyond **N**everland's **r**ed **m**achines.)

- Have students individually or in groups do in-depth research of a particular style and write a paper, create a model or diorama, or give a presentation to the class. If students create models, you could host a class city tour for parents, with students walking parents through their "cities," describing the architecture and the time periods represented.

- Expand the study to include architectural styles from non-Western cultures.

- Create a memory game using duplicate images of architectural styles and elements and pasting them on cardboard or construction paper to create cards. (Students shuffle them face down, then take turns flipping two cards at a time. If they flip a matched set, they keep the pair and take another turn. If the cards don't match, they flip them back over and another student takes a turn.)

History of Architecture

Name:_____

Draw a simple version of each of these architectural styles.

Egyptian	Greek	Roman
Romanesque	Gothic	Renaissance
Baroque	Neoclassical	Romantic
Modern	Other styles you like	

120

Chapter 13
Renaissance and Baroque Art

Reason vs. Emotion

— Pat Hollingsworth —

Renaissance and Baroque Art

The Renaissance and Baroque periods are two of the most important eras for American history. The Renaissance was the time of the discoveries of Columbus and other explorers. The Baroque period was the heyday of monarchies that led directly to the American Revolution. It is important for students to make those interdisciplinary connections, and through active learning, the connections come to life as students consider the real people and lives that are beyond the often dry facts of history. This lesson enables students to understand how values and ideals influence the art, architecture, and events of a culture.

Materials

- ☐ books about or art prints by Renaissance artists: Sandro Botticelli, Leonardo da Vinci, Michelangelo (see, for example, Whiting 1998)

- ☐ books about or art prints by Baroque artists: Peter Paul Rubens, Michelangelo Merisi da Caravaggio, Artemisia Gentileschi, Gian Lorenzo Bernini (see, for example, Neret 2004, Toman 1998)

- ☐ Renaissance vs. Baroque Graphic Organizer (page 124)

- ☐ Renaissance or Baroque-era costume

- ☐ student flow journals (see page 7)

Preparation

1. Choose an artist or related figure from either period to act out for the class, such as Leonardo da Vinci (see page 123). Costumes do not need to be elaborate. Hats, scarves, and long skirts for women capture the idea, once you begin your first-person narrative. For Leonardo, a scarf wrapped around the head, black pants, silk or velvet-type shirt hanging over pants, serving as an artist smock, and a paint brush completes the costume.

2. Photocopy the Renaissance vs. Baroque Graphic Organizer (page 124) for each student.

Getting Students Excited about the Topic

When the teacher arrives in class dressed as Mona Lisa, Leonardo da Vinci, Peter Paul Rubens, or Artemesia Gentileschi, students get interested and pay attention. Actually, any person from the period would work just as well. Begin by introducing yourself:

❝*My name is Leonardo da Vinci. I am a very famous artist from the Renaissance period. The Renaissance was a rebirth of ideas from classical Greece and Rome. Classical ideals that were followed in the Renaissance were balance and reason—in other words, 'nothing to excess.' My painting of* Mona Lisa *is a good example of Renaissance balance and restraint. You will notice that I did not give her a big smile like some of the Baroque artists do.*

The Baroque period that followed the Renaissance was a time of exuberance that emphasized emotions. Ruben's Daniel in the Lion's Den *is a good example of Baroque emotion and movement. It is oozing with emotion, not only of Daniel but also of the lions. Personally, I think Baroque art is excessive.*

*You will have your chance to compare and contrast these two periods. I hope you will think favorably about the rational, balanced, and restrained aspects of Renaissance art.***❞**

Guided Practice

1. Share the objectives with students so that they can relate to the learning ahead.

2. Show artwork from the artists listed above. Help students to see the characteristic differences in the art of the two periods. Use the following as a guide:

Renaissance	**Baroque**
restrained subjects	exuberant subjects
stillness	movement, swirling
natural light	dramatic light
rationality	emotion
dignity	excitement

Although not every Renaissance or Baroque artwork will have these characteristics, these are the most salient features of the art of those times.

3. Ask students to identify verbally any characteristics of the two styles that they recognize in the art prints or books.

4. Call upon individual students to dramatize each of the characteristics. Ask them to identify whether the characteristic is Renaissance or Baroque. This can be done silently or with sounds.

5. Hand out a graphic organizer for each student to compare the styles.

DISTINCT RENAISSANCE CHARACTERISTICS	SIMILAR CHARACTERISTICS	DISTINCT BAROQUE CHARACTERISTICS

Independent Practice

1. Ask students, "What are the major differences between Renaissance and Baroque art?" and write a few answers on the board before having students get into pairs to share their completed organizers.

2. Ask all students to do a quick (10-minute) writing assignment in which they defend one of these art styles as being superior to the other.

3. Then ask one or two students to share aloud before everyone goes back to verbal sharing with the same partners.

First-Person Narratives

Have students research Renaissance artists Sandro Botticelli, Leonardo da Vinci, or Michelangelo and Baroque artist, Peter Paul Rubens, Caravaggio,

LET'S RAP ABOUT THE RENAISSANCE

Artemisia Gentileschi, or Gian Lorenzo Bernini and write a short first-person narrative from the perspective of one of the artists, based on the research and the distinguishing characteristics of each period. The narratives should emphasize the prominent characteristics of the period.

Open-Ended Tasks

1. Write the following choices on the board.

   Group 1. Create a skit to extol the virtues of Renaissance art.
   Group 2. Create a skit to extol the virtues of Baroque art.
   Group 3. Create a song, chant, or rap to demonstrate differences between Renaissance and Baroque art.
   Group 4. Create a song, chant, or rap to laud Renaissance art.
   Group 5. Create a song, chant, or rap to laud Baroque art.

2. Ask students to express interest in a group, then select four or five students for each group, depending on the size of your class.

3. Have students work until near the end of class. Let them know that they will have half of the next class time to finish the project and that they should bring costumes or props to that class.

4. Each presentation should be between five and eight minutes long.

5. Grade groups using the Presentations Rubric on page 127.

Closure

The closure for this lesson will be students' presentations of projects during class. End by saying how much the students have learned about the influence that values have on a culture's art, architecture, and events.

Evaluation

Evaluate project presentations with the Presentations Rubric (page127).

Reflection

- Ask students to share examples of how they reached the goals of this lesson. This could be an oral discussion or a writing assignment.

- Discuss with your students any aspects of flow that they experienced and add the information to the class flow chart (see page 5). Then ask students to make entries in their flow journals (see page 7).

Extension

Give homework assignments based on student choice, enabling students to decide whether to do an assignment that uses their strengths or to challenge themselves to develop new strengths. Using specific examples of Renaissance and Baroque artwork, students select a homework assignment from the following:

- Draw or paint examples of one or both styles and write paragraphs explaining the salient characteristics of the styles.

- Write a poem about one or both styles.

- Write a short essay comparing the styles. (For example, "Compare Michelangelo's *David* with Bernini's *David,* then select the one you believe to be the better artwork and defend your reasoning.")

- Create a computer slide presentation (such as Power Point) about one or both art styles.

Give students rubrics, deadlines, and guidelines on the approximate length of the presentation. Keep presentations short to hold audience interest (about five minutes).

Presentations Rubric

Name:_____ Date:_____

Presentations will be self-evaluated and teacher-evaluated.

	0	1	2	3	Points
Knowledge of subject matter	Does not show knowledge gained	Shows some understanding of the two periods	Shows good understanding of the two periods	Excellent command of facts; outstanding analysis of characteristics of the two styles	
Planning and execution of project	Did not complete or lacked planning	Shows some planning and follow-through; prompting needed	Well planned	Extremely well planned and organized; independently executed	
Creativity	Did not complete	Shows some fluency	Shows fluency and flexibility	Shows fluency, flexibility, originality, and elaboration	
Presentation	Did not complete	Emerging presentation skills	Proficient presentation skills; clear and understandable	Extremely clear, understandable, interesting presentation	
				Total Points:	

Scoring:
10–12 points: Outstanding
7–9 points: Well done
4–6 points: Satisfactory
0–3 points: Unsatisfactory

Part Three

Active Learning Everywhere

Chapter 14
Create a Unique Dictionary

Active Learning of Vocabulary and
Dictionary Skills

— Stacy Hale —

Create a Unique Dictionary

"Man, I've never looked at the dictionary so much before!" Ryan, an eighth-grader, tells his classmate, Tyler. "Some of these words are pretty cool." This class is working on a "unique dictionary," a compilation of words they choose that requires hands-on use of the dictionary, creative-thinking skills, and writing sentences using contextual structure. Students choose one word for each letter of the alphabet and, depending on age and skill, write the part of speech and definitions, illustrate the word in some form, and write a sentence using the word correctly in context. Students may work individually, in pairs, or in small groups; younger students may do just one word apiece for a class dictionary. The dictionary can be either a short-term or a long-term assignment. The ultimate goal is to get the students excited about new words and familiar with the layout of a dictionary. Once they are familiar, they will be less intimidated by the dictionary and more likely to use it.

Materials

- ☐ approx. six or seven 8½" x 11" sheets of paper per student
- ☐ long-reach stapler
- ☐ various colors of construction paper for a cover
- ☐ crayons, colored pencils, glue, scissors, and other craft materials (Warning: Colored markers tend to bleed through to the next page)
- ☐ different types of magazines for illustrations
- ☐ scissors for students
- ☐ any type of standard dictionary
- ☐ student flow journals (see page 7)

Grades: 1–8

Time Frame Options

- Older or advanced students: 26 lessons, 30 minutes each
- Younger students and beginning readers: one 30-minute lesson

Measurable Learning Objectives

Share these aims with students:

- Students will choose one word for each letter in the alphabet and write the parts of speech and definitions.
- Intermediate students will also illustrate the words using a creative device or appropriate pictures.
- Advanced students will also write an original sentence using the words correctly in context.

Preparation

1. Fold six or seven sheets of paper in half and staple along the center to create a booklet. If you teach primarily beginning readers and writers, six sheets should be more than enough (they might skip the letter *X*, for example). Create a booklet for each student (or group of students, if they will work together).

2. Prepare examples on 8½" x 11" paper: "*A* is for adze," for example. One example should demonstrate that the drawn pictures do not have to be detailed, just able to convey the word's meaning. Create another example of a word illustrated with a picture from a magazine. To demonstrate using a creative device, choose a word that can be illustrated with texture, such as a small braid of yarn for the word "queue," or illustrated with manipulation, such as "*I* is for infinitesimal (infinitesimal).

Getting Students Excited about the Topic

1. Introduce the topic with an interesting new vocabulary word. For example:

   > **"** *Did you ever notice how much time you spend in class just boondoggling? Do you know what 'boondoggle' means? It basically means looking busy doing nothing. You would be amazed at some of the words in the dictionary.* **"**

2. Explain the objectives to students so that they understand and can relate to the learning goals. Tell them they will create a unique dictionary full of words that they choose.

   > **"** *Remember alphabet books that said, 'A is for apple, B is for boy?' Your dictionary is going to say something like 'A is for ankh, B is for Baroque.' You are going to use the dictionary to find the most unusual words you can. Then you may illustrate the words using pictures out of magazines, drawings with crayons or colored pencils, or some other way to show your word's meaning. When you're done with the dictionary, you will make a cover with a title and your name on it.* **"**

Guided Practice

Show students the examples of completed letters you prepared. Encourage them to choose words that can be easily illustrated.

Independent Practice

1. Have students make a word list to be approved by you to avoid inappropriate words or words that are too simplistic. Students having difficulty choosing words may need individual guidance. The letters *X, Y,* and *Z* have very limited choices, so one option is to use only one of the letters instead of all three.

2. Some students may wish to have a theme for their dictionary. One student did a sports dictionary, with every word related in some way to sports, while another did a love dictionary, filled with adjectives describing love and romance.

3. After their word lists are approved, students take the dictionary booklets and begin labeling each page with its letter, starting with *A* on the front page. Students then write the word on each letter's page, its part of speech, and its definitions.

4. Students illustrate each word with hand-drawn pictures, pictures cut from magazines, computer-generated artwork, or some other creative device. Creative devices may include manipulating how the word itself is written or using additional materials such as yarn, glitter, felt, or cloth. One student used "*R* is for recumbent" and drew all the letters lying down. Another student used "*B* is for braille" and outlined the word with small pinpricks to give it a raised-dot feel. Challenge your advanced students to use creative devices for the illustrations.

5. Advanced students then write a sentence using each word in context. The sentence should contain contextual clues that underscore the word's meaning. Students should avoid sentences like "My dog is lethargic." Demonstrate how details added to the sentence can tell the reader what the word means. "My dog is so lethargic he eats lying down and falls asleep with his head in the bowl." Encourage students to read their sentences to each other to see if they have provided clues to their word's meaning.

6. Students create a cover for their finished dictionary, with their dictionary title and their name on it. They decorate the cover with pictures, drawings, and any other materials they like.

Closure

Either in small groups or as a class, pass around the completed dictionaries. Students enjoy seeing each other's work and critiquing word choice and illustrations. They are also exposed to new words, complete with definitions and illustrations.

Evaluation

- Dictionary evaluation is determined by various factors: length of assignment, page requirements, grammatical accuracy, and so forth. Grade illustrations on ability to communicate meaning, not on artistic ability. A simple stick-figure drawing can accurately portray a word's meaning. You could give extra credit for creative devices.

- Grade contextual sentences on students' ability to communicate meaning. This is an excellent area for student participation. Students as a class can help evaluate sentences, determining if the sentence correctly conveys the word's meaning. Read the sentence to the class and then ask if students know what the chosen word means based on the sentence's content. Have them assign a point value to the sentence:

  1 for poor content
  2 for fair content
  3 for good content
  4 for excellent content

- Grammatical requirements could also be assigned. Misspelled words, incorrect parts of speech, or incomplete definitions could all result in point reductions. The easiest way to grade the assignment is to determine points possible per letter.

One word only: Students were required to do only one word.

25 points possible for word choice

25 points possible for part of speech and definitions

50 points possible for illustration and context sentences

A–X, Y, or Z: Students were required to do 24 words, A through W, then either X, Y, or Z

1 point per letter for word choice

1 point per letter for part of speech and definition

2 points for illustration and/or context sentence

= 96 points total, with 4 additional points possible for either word list or cover

Reflection

- Ask students to share examples of how they reached the goals of this lesson. This could be an oral discussion or a writing assignment.

- Discuss with your students any aspects of flow that they experienced and add the information to the class flow chart (see page 5). Then ask students to make entries in their flow journals (see page 7).

Extension

Adapt the idea to particular terminology students need to learn in science, history, math, art, or any subject. Students each define, use, describe, and illustrate one term for a class dictionary, or each student creates a terminology booklet of all terms on a list you supply.

Chapter 15

Become the Adverb

Active Learning in Language Arts

— Gina Lewis —

Become the Adverb

L earning the parts of speech can become more than just memorizing definitions when students *become* the parts of speech! Once you have been an adverb in the parts of speech game, you will always remember how an adverb works. This oral and kinesthetic activity makes learning fun.

> **Grades: 1–8**
>
> **Time Frame Options**
> *40 to 45 minutes*
>
> **Measurable Learning Objectives**
> Share these aims with students:
> - *Students will create visual sentences by using their bodies to become the eight parts of speech.*
> - *Students will create written sentences using the eight parts of speech.*

Materials

- ☐ craft sticks (more than one per student)
- ☐ felt-tip pens
- ☐ grab bag
- ☐ pencil and paper for each student
- ☐ student flow journals (see page 7)

Preparation

Prepare the craft sticks by writing the eight parts of speech on them (noun, verb, adjective, adverb, pronoun, preposition, conjunction, and interjection), one part per stick, repeatedly, until you run out of sticks. Put them all in the grab bag.

 ## Getting Students Excited about the Topic

1. Explain the gist of the activity and the goals students will achieve, then have students draw a stick from the grab bag:

   66 *Today we are going to practice being the parts of speech that we have learned. One at a time, you will draw a stick from the bag. The part of speech on that stick is what you will be for today's lesson.* **99**

2. Have students choose partners from other students with the same part of speech. Together, they brainstorm as many words as they can for their part of speech and write the words down.

DOING MY PART!

Guided Practice

1. Explain that students will build visual sentences using their bodies. Start by asking a noun to come forward, then continue with other parts of speech. For example:

> 66 *What noun are you? Dog. Okay, now I need a verb to come forward. What verb are you? Ran. How about an adverb to modify this verb? Quickly. We now have the most basic sentence. Dog ran quickly or Dog quickly ran. Let's continue to improve our sentence.* 99

2. Be sure to continue this activity until everyone has had at least one turn. Create as many types of sentences as you can. Use this time for discussion and instruction. For example:

> 66 *Remember that the adjective will qualify the noun or pronoun. What will the adverb modify?* 99

Independent Practice

Students divide into small groups and create sentences by contributing the part of speech that they have become for this lesson. They will then write the ones that they think are best, labeling each part of speech, for turning in and sharing with the class.

Closure

Review with students the rules of a complete sentence: It must make sense and have a subject, a verb, a capital letter at the beginning, and an ending punctuation mark. Have students review their papers again to make sure the sentences are complete.

Evaluation

Grade the sentences using the following criteria or your own:

At least five complete sentences (extra credit for additional)

All eight parts of speech represented within sentences

Correct labeling of eight parts of speech

Cooperation among team members

Reflection

- Ask students to share examples of how they reached the goals of this lesson. This could be an oral discussion or a writing assignment.

- Discuss with your students any aspects of flow that they experienced and add the information to the class flow chart (see page 5). Then ask students to make entries in their flow journals (see page 7).

Extension

- Modify this lesson whenever students need to memorize definitions.

- Use this lesson as a part of foreign language instruction.

Chapter 16

Word Works

Active Reading and Writing
for Young Children

— Pat Hollingsworth —

Word Works

Grades: PreK–2

Time Frame Options

15 to 20 minutes daily
with each group of five
to seven children

Measurable Learning Objectives

Share these aims with
students:

- Beginning students will
  be able to read and
  trace their own names
  and words.
- Intermediate students
  will read and write their
  own sentences.
- Advanced students will
  write their own para-
  graphs.

Both reading and writing can be active when students are mentally engaged and physically involved in their learning. As soon as five-year-old Matt enters the kindergarten room, he enthusiastically says, "Today I want my new word to be Superman." His mind is filled with images and ideas. Ages four and five are ideal times for children to develop their fine motor skills, particularly handwriting, and to begin learning to read at the same time.

With Word Works, you ask children each day what new words they would like to learn, then write each selected word on an index card for the children to keep in their individual folders. Each day, the children read their cards, trace them, and then get a new word of their choice. Word Works is easiest to do with individual students or with small groups of five or six students, but you could do it with a whole class, once the procedure is established.

Materials

- [ ] 500 or more 5" x 8" cards
- [ ] folder for each child
- [ ] several reams of lightweight white typing paper
- [ ] thick felt-tip pens (all colors except yellow, which is too light)
- [ ] student flow journals (see page 7)

Preparation

1. Write each child's name on a folder.

2. Write each child's name in the top left of an index card. You will need one of these per child, per day, so you might create several in advance for each child.

Getting Students Excited about the Topic

1. Introduce Word Works by explaining it as a way for children to have fun with words and learn more about what they already love. Explain the goals so that students can understand them and are excited about achieving them. For example:

> 66 *We are going to begin something called Word Works. Think of the names of all the people you love. Think of the names of all the things that you like to do. When we do reading and writing together, you will get to select who and what you will study. Learning to read and write is great fun. You can have any word that you want. You can have as many words as you want. You can pick short words, long words, hard words, easy words. The choice is yours. Soon you will be writing your own sentences and stories.* 99

2. Explain that every day you will write each child's name in the top left corner of a 5" x 8" card. The child will then tell you a word (or, later, a sentence) that he or she wants to write. Write that word on the card and give it to the student to trace on white typing paper.

Guided Practice—Day 1

1. Begin the first day by explaining carefully how the children should trace the new words:

> 66 *Now I want each of you to tell me one word that you want to learn today. After I have given you a word and you have read it back to me, I want you to trace your name and your word at the top of a sheet of typing paper. I want you to trace over your name and your word carefully, just the way I have written it, even if you know how to write it yourself. I want you to learn this particular way to write the words.* 99

2. Then explain that you will give students additional words after everyone has finished tracing one word.

> 66 *When everyone has received and written one word, I will begin giving you more words to add to your sheet of paper. At the end of our working time today, I want you to put all your 5" x 8" cards in your folder so that you will have them for tomorrow.* 99

Guided Practice—Day 2

The next day, begin by having students review the previous day's words, reading them to the whole group and tracing them again as a review.

❝ *First, get out your word cards from yesterday. Before we begin writing, I want you each to read the words you wrote yesterday to the whole group. After reading your words, I want you to begin tracing your name and your words, just as you did yesterday. I will begin giving new words to students who have carefully traced their names and words from yesterday.* **❞**

Independent Practice

1. By the third day, students will know the procedure and be able to independently get their folders, read their words to the group, and begin writing their words. The amount of time spent on individual words will vary according to the age and ability of the group. Preschool children will probably need to write in this way all year. Kindergartners may need to write in this way for five or six months. Older children might require much less time using this system with individual words.

2. As student abilities grow, some students will begin asking for sentences. These can be done just as the individual words were done. As students master the handwriting and reading, they will begin to want to write more complicated sentences and paragraphs. Generally, there is a gentle flow from tracing words to writing sentences independently.

Closure

At group time, each child may read what he or she wrote during Word Works. This closure provides time to share with the whole group, to reinforce the reading of words, and to practice speaking in front of a group.

Evaluation

Each day's work is an evaluation. Use the Writing and Reading Rubric (page 145) once a month and keep the rubrics to record progress.

Reflection

- Ask students to share examples of how they reached the goals of this lesson. This could be an oral discussion or a writing assignment.

- Discuss with your students any aspects of flow that they experienced and add the information to the class flow chart (see page 5). Then ask students to make entries in their flow journals (see page 7).

Extension

Continue to use this technique as students advance in their reading and writing skills. Encourage students to choose their own reading and writing assignments by telling you what they are interested in reading or writing about each day, week, or month. Supply individual reading and writing assigments based on interest and the curriculum as much as possible.

Writing and Reading Rubric

Name: _____ Date: _____

	0	1	2	3	Points
Student writes name legibly.	Not legible	Legible but letters are very uneven	Legible but all caps	Legible; uses uppercase and lower-case letters appropriately	
Student can read the words he or she has chosen.	Cannot read any of the words	Can read about 25 to 50 percent of the words	Can read about 50 to 75 percent of the words	Can read about 75 to 100 percent of the words	
Student writes the words legibly.	No legible words	About 25 to 50 percent are legible	About 50 to 75 percent are legible	About 75 to 100 percent are legible	
				Total Points:	

Scoring:
9 = Excellent
8 = Very good
7 = Good
6 = Average
5 and below = Needs improvement

Chapter 17

Charlotte's Web Reading Unit

Active Learning in Classic Literature

— Gina Lewis —

Charlotte's Web Reading Unit

The children's literature classic *Charlotte's Web,* by E. B. White, is an important component of the literature program. Along with being an enjoyable reading experience for students, *Charlotte's Web* will fulfill the task of studying the fiction genre and themes relevant to an elementary grade–level experience. The students are exposed to various reading, writing, responding, and studying strategies as they progress through this delightful story in which animals talk and children, just like the students reading about them, are involved in learning important life lessons. An assortment of enrichment activities will bring this project to life for students. *Charlotte's Web* is a way to educate elementary-age children in the cognitive, affective, and psychomotor domains, because it lends itself to activities that employ all three areas of development.

Materials

- ☐ copies of the book *Charlotte's Web* for all students
- ☐ copies of *Charlotte's Web* Daily Reading Journal (page 151), enough for each student to have one for each chapter
- ☐ copies of the three comprehensive worksheets on pages 152–154 for each student
- ☐ pencil and paper for each student
- ☐ construction paper
- ☐ markers, paints, or colored pencils
- ☐ *Charlotte's Web* VHS or DVD and a player
- ☐ student flow journals (see page 7)

Preparation

1. Photocopy the reading journal and worksheets at the end of this chapter. Be sure to make enough copies of the journal to give each student one journal sheet per chapter in the book.

Grades: 2–4

Time Frame Options
- First three weeks: 30 to 40 minutes daily
- Fourth week: 1 hour daily

Measurable Learning Objectives
Share these aims with students:
- Students will identify the major elements of story structure: characters, setting, and plot.
- Students will experience cooperative reading, independent reading, and listening skills related to reading.
- Students will develop study and test-taking skills pertinent to reading development.
- Students will create dramas, products, and reading journals.
- Students will complete worksheets and a final exam for evaluation.

2. Brainstorm ideas for props that you can provide, or ask students to bring in items related to the themes in the book.

3. Combine all worksheet questions into a comprehensive test to give students at the end of the unit.

 # Getting Students Excited about the Topic

1. Introduce the topic by discussing pets and favorite animals. Give each child time to talk about his or her pets or favorite animals.

> **❝** *How do you think that we communicate with animals? Do you think that animals communicate with one another? Today we will begin reading a book about animals that talk.* **❞**

2. Hand out the books and encourage students to look at the cover and the pictures, and discuss the author, copyright date, and any questions or thoughts the students have.

3. Explain the aims of the lesson so that students understand and can relate to what they will achieve. Tell students that each day they will read one chapter, which is approximately 10–12 pages of the book. Any reading they do not finish in class will be homework.

4. Let students know that once they have finished reading the book, they will do activities, take a test, and watch a movie about the book.

Guided Practice

On the first day, the whole class examines the book and discusses the author:

> **❝** *E. B. White also wrote* The Trumpet of the Swan *and* Stuart Little. *All his children's books have won many awards. E. B. stands for Elwyn Brooks. In 1978, he received a special citation from the Pulitzer Prize Committee for his outstanding literary contributions.* **❞**

Independent Practice

1. During the first three weeks, on Monday through Thursday, students will read one chapter per day and write about the chapter on the *Charlotte's*

Web Daily Reading Journal (page 151). Additionally, the class could create a spelling and vocabulary list based on words they each record on the journaling sheet.

2. Vary the reading so that students read as a class on Mondays, with a partner on Tuesdays, independently on Wednesdays, and with a different partner on Thursdays.

3. Book discussions on Fridays will focus on the plot of the most recently read material. After the discussion, students will complete a worksheet that will prepare them for the comprehensive test (worksheet 1, on page 152, on the first Friday; worksheet 2, on page 153, on the second Friday; and worksheet 3, on page 154, on the third Friday). Make sure students keep the three graded worksheets because the comprehensive test comes directly from them. Possible book discussion prompts:

> **Week 1:** *We will discuss how Wilbur and Fern felt when Wilbur had to leave and go to the Zuckermans' farm. Has anyone in this class ever had to move or change schools? How does that feel? Do you think people adjust to changes easily? What could people do to help other people make changes like that?*

> **Week 2:** *Today we will discuss all of the friends that Wilbur made and how they helped him. What do you think of the goose? The sheep? Templeton? Fern? Charlotte? Are they good friends? Are they all the same? How would Wilbur's life had been different without his friends? Think of your friends and the type of friend that you are. Which character in the book is most like you? Why?*

> **Week 3:** *Our book discussion today will focus on Wilbur and Charlotte. I want us to discuss how they became best friends even though they are so different. How are they alike?*

4. During the fourth week, plan a different activity for each day:

> **Monday**—The students will write a new ending to the book to practice writing fictional prose. They will then share it with the class.

> **Tuesday**—The students will create artwork illustrating scenes from the beginning, middle, and end of the book. Post this artwork around the room or in the hall.

> **Wednesday**—The students will pick scenes from the book to perform as short dramatizations, either independently or cooperatively.

> **Thursday**—Have students complete a comprehensive test that you create from the worksheets.

> **Friday**—The students who passed the test with a 75% or above will view the animated movie of *Charlotte's Web*. Those who did not pass will retest before viewing the remainder of the movie.

Closure

Once the students have presented their creations and performances, have them write summaries of their experiences and the important things they learned about friendship and other relationships.

Evaluation

■ Periodically assess students' progress by checking their daily journals to make sure they have not fallen behind in their reading. The journaling could be assessed for completeness and effort.

■ Grade products and performances based on following directions and completing work on time, neatness, creativity, and quality and depth of information.

■ Grade the three worksheets and final exam using the answer sheet (page 155).

Reflection

■ Ask students to share examples of how they reached the goals of this lesson. This could be an oral discussion or a writing assignment.

■ Discuss with your students any aspects of flow that they experienced and add the information to the class flow chart (see page 5). Then ask students to make entries in their flow journals (see page 7).

Extension

■ **Library assignment:** Have students choose one of the animals in the story and find a book in the library about it. They then write an expository paragraph about the factual animal that the character represents. For example: A student who chooses Wilbur would write an informative, factual paragraph about pigs.

■ **Field trips:** Arrange a visit to a university entomology department, if possible, as well as a visit to a zoo or farm to view firsthand the animals represented in the book. Be sure to plan far ahead, contact the right people, schedule the bus, and create permission slips. If you plan on reading several books about animals throughout the year, the field trips could relate to more than just this one book.

Charlotte's Web
Daily Reading Journal

Name: _____ Date: _____

Chapter: _____

My response to this chapter is

_____

_____

_____

_____

_____

Words in this chapter that are new to me:

_____

_____

_____

_____

_____

_____

Charlotte's Web Worksheet 1

Name: _____ Date: _____

Simple Recall

Fill in the blank.

1. Name the author of this book.

_____

2. Name the title and copyright date of this book.

_____

3. Who is the main character?

_____

4. Who are the secondary characters?

_____

5. What is the setting?

_____

Multiple Choice

Underline the correct answer.

1. At the very beginning of the story, several (pigs, ducks, spiders) were born during the first night.

2. (Fern, Avery, Mr. Zuckerman) rescued Wilbur from certain death and adopted him as a pet.

3. Avery carried a (gun, sword, drum) and a wooden dagger.

4. When Wilbur got too big to be a pet, he was sold to (Homer Zuckerman, Mrs. Arable, Charlotte).

5. (Charlotte, Templeton, the goose) turned out to be Wilbur's best friend at the new farm.

Charlotte's Web Worksheet 2

Name: _____ Date: ___ _____

True or False

Write a T for true or an F for false next to each statement.

_____ 1. Mr. Arable planned to kill the runt.

_____ 2. Wilbur was very large at birth.

_____ 3. Fern thought Wilbur was not beautiful.

_____ 4. Fern loved having the pig for a pet.

_____ 5. Wilbur had trouble sleeping.

_____ 6. Templeton was a quiet, polite rat.

_____ 7. Charlotte was trying to save Wilbur.

_____ 8. Seven goslings hatched.

_____ 9. Charlotte wove her web in the barn.

_____ 10. Mr. Zuckerman was Fern's grandfather.

Matching

Write the letter of the description next to the character it describes.

_____ 1. Fern   A. Bought Wilbur when he became too big to be a pet

_____ 2. Avery   B. Helped Charlotte get to the fair in his mouth

_____ 3. Mr. Arable   C. Had seven goslings

_____ 4. Mrs. Arable   D. Fern's father

_____ 5. Mr. Zuckerman   E. Fern's mother

_____ 6. Wilbur   F. Fern's brother

_____ 7. Charlotte   G. Loved Wilbur very much and kept him for a pet

_____ 8. Templeton   H. Told Wilbur he would be killed

_____ 9. Sheep   I. Wove fantastic webs to save a friend's life

_____ 10. Goose   J. Won an award at the county fair

Charlotte's Web Worksheet 3

Name: _____ Date: _____

Essay

Write at least five complete sentences explaining how Wilbur and Charlotte are alike.

_____

_____

_____

_____

_____

_____

_____

Write at least five complete sentences explaining how Wilbur and Charlotte are different.

_____

_____

_____

_____

_____

_____

_____

Charlotte's Web
Answer Sheet for Worksheets

Simple Recall

1. E. B. White
2. Charlotte's Web, 1980 (may vary depending on edition used)
3. Wilbur
4. Charlotte, Fern, Templeton
5. A farm

Multiple Choice

1. Pigs
2. Fern
3. Gun
4. Homer Zuckerman
5. Charlotte

True or False

1. T
2. F
3. F
4. T
5. T
6. F
7. T
8. T
9. T
10. F

Matching

1. G
2. F
3. D
4. E
5. A
6. J
7. I
8. B
9. H
10. C

Chapter 18
Take the Fear Out

Active Learning in Writing

— Katie Abercrombie —

Take the Fear Out

Grades: 1–8

Time Frame Options

- Prewriting: 1 hour
- Subsequent days: 30 to 40 minutes a day

Measurable Learning Objectives

Share these aims with students:

- Students will become familiar with a variety of prewriting, idea-gathering techniques.
- Students will be able to compose quickly when the writing step begins.
- Students will use specific details when writing.

Fear is the number-one enemy of writing. It paralyzes us as we stare at the blank space on a computer screen or sheet of paper. But the simple truth is that if you can talk, you can write. Writing is simply "talking" transferred to paper.

Vivid and active writing brings an added bonus. Active learning, besides getting us started writing, puts content into the writer's mind. Suddenly sentences are filled with interesting, specific, "rainbow" details instead of boring, say-nothing, "gray" words. One of the biggest problems in student writing—content too general—is magically fixed.

This lesson follows an ancient Egypt unit, after a period of study, as an example to spark the imagination of the students; however, the technique could be used to describe any subject matter, from a walk in the woods to listening to Maya Angelou read her poetry.

Materials

- ☐ paper and pencils for students
- ☐ overhead projector or class board
- ☐ copy of photo or drawing of subject for each student (drawing of Egyptian pyramid builders in this lesson example)
- ☐ student flow journals (see page 7)
- ☐ audiotape or CD of soft instrumental music

Preparation

Choose and photocopy the photo or drawing of the subject for each student. To follow the example in this lesson, draw or find an image of Egyptian pyramid builders.

Getting Students Excited about the Topic

1. Engage students in the idea of becoming someone else through writing. For example:

   > *Tomorrow we are going to jump inside history and become Egyptian pyramid builders. You are going to write a first-person narrative—a diary entry—about your experience. You've been studying about Egypt in social studies, and now we're actually going to 'live' in this period. Your homework assignment tonight is to find five to ten facts about the pyramids that you can share with the class. Your sources can be the encyclopedia, the Internet, a history text, or notes from your unit lectures. Be ready tomorrow to time travel.*

2. Explain the aims of the lesson to students so that they understand and can relate to the learning objectives and how they will benefit them. Tell students that fear stops many of us from writing, even though writing is no more than talking transferred to paper. Encourage them to think of their hands as tools:

   > *Think about it. We do not really write with our hands. We hear the words and write with our ears. Our hands are simply tools. The only job for our fingers is to copy ideas that are already in our minds and on our lips.*

3. Explain that writing is really a two-step process: (1) Prewriting—deciding what to say (our minds and lips); and (2) Writing—saying it (our hands). Point out that writing is scary when we try to do both steps at the same time.

   > *Deciding what to say—'talking'—takes away the fear of the actual writing step. And that's where active learning comes into play. 'Talking' is a synonym for prewriting activities, when we decide what to say. These activities could include talking to a partner out loud or to yourself in the form of thinking. However, 'talking' could also include many other activities, such as researching the topic, acting out the subject with mime, drawing the scene to live within the details, or imagining the situation and making lists of sensory words.*

Guided Practice

1. Encourage students to start with the facts by sharing one fact about the topic while you write the facts on an overhead transparency or on the board. (The overhead is better than the board because it can be used for review if the assignment takes more than one class period.)

2. Students continue adding facts until everyone's list of facts is used up. The history lesson itself is then basically student-taught, with you filling in missing information at the end.

3. Next, students will start prewriting. Pass out the copy of a drawing of workers at an Egyptian pyramid and provide students a few minutes to look closely at the picture. (While the subject for this lesson example is ancient Egypt, the topic could be anything. The image could be a palm-lined, white sandy beach with deep blue water beyond. Or it might be of gorillas in the wild. The method is the same. Make it something that can be felt and written about vividly.)

4. Ask students to focus on one worker in the drawing. Have them close their eyes and create a movie scene, visualizing what that person's life was like.

5. Next, students could try any of the prewriting activities that follow before they actually start the writing assignment.

Prewriting Options

MIME

Use any subject matter that is relevant to the class for a miming activity. The activity is most effective with a well-thought-out and rehearsed script.

Today we are going to take a journey back in time. Everyone stand up and spread out. It is 4,000 years ago, and you are an Egyptian worker. It is noon, and you have been working since sunrise. Wipe your brow because sweat is pouring down your face.

Look up at the hot, burning sun high in the sky. Squint and shade your eyes because it is so bright. How does your body feel? Move and stretch as we focus on each part. Think about the muscles in your back. (Pause) *Think about your arms and legs.* (Pause) *You are probably barefoot. Feel your feet on the hard, hot, gritty path.* (Pause) *Think about your skin.* (Pause) *What does the sun feel like?* (Pause) *Is there a wind?* (Pause)

You are on a work crew hauling a huge stone block up a ramp to the top of a pyramid. Line up four in a group. The leader of each group needs to mime the edges of the stone so that everyone knows how big the stone is that they are hauling. Now every member of the groups needs to grab the rope. Feel the hard, twisted twine against the palm of your hand. Now pull in unison. Really tug. This stone is so heavy. It barely moves with each tug. (Pause while groups struggle to move the stone. Encourage them to tense their muscles and fight that stone. Make sure groups are pulling together.)

Your group stops to rest and look around. (Pause) *You are standing right next to the stone block. Look up at it and study it.* (Pause) *What does it look like? Touch it.* (Pause) *Now look over at your fellow workers. Really observe them.* (Pause) *What do the other workers say or do?* (Pause)

You look across the desert from your construction site. What do you see? (Pause) *Are there any other pyramids, or is your construction by itself?* (Pause) *What different shapes are all around you?* (Pause) *Do you taste or smell anything as you take this rest?* (Pause) *Sit down for a moment. What does it feel like?* (Pause)

The foreman yells at your group to get back to work. Everyone picks up the rope and starts to heave and pull. (Pause) *You look at the slope of the ramp ahead. You look above at where this stone has to eventually end up. What are you thinking?*

Have students sit quietly for 60 seconds and ponder what just happened. Then move to the writing assignment.

DRAWING

If drawing is involved in a writing assignment, most teachers ask students to complete the written part and then illustrate it as a final step. This approach does not use the visual part of the brain to gather ideas and details to help the writing. Often, if you draw first and write last, then backwards is really forwards!

Sometimes students balk at this assignment, complaining that they are not good artists. Your job is to bring a comfort level to the assignment, explaining that the drawing does not have to be a work of art. Instead, it is an aid to thinking. In fact, often the artist "sees" a lot more in the drawing than an outsider because the imagination is "seeing" much more than appears on paper. No problem. When the artist begins writing, these invisible details will appear in words.

To apply this prewriting option to the Egyptian lesson, you would follow the class discussion of pyramid facts with a study of the handout picture. Then have students draw a scene focusing on one worker. Soft instrumental music might be played in the classroom and a short time limit announced ahead of time for the assignment—five or ten minutes. This is not an art project, just an idea-gathering tool.

At the end, students should pair off and explain to a partner what the drawing is about—give each person 60 seconds. When students are asked to "talk" about their drawing, guess what? The first step in writing has just been completed. Then tell students to pick up their pencils and write what they have been saying out loud. This begins the writing assignment. If you notice a student seems to be stuck and is staring at the blank page, ask the student to draw again for 60 seconds and then return to the writing. Repeat this until the writing flow gets started, but monitor the student. Don't let the student get so involved in drawing that the writing assignment somehow never happens.

Drawing can be an extremely powerful writing tool. I have done this assignment with adults, asking them to draw a favorite childhood memory and then write about it. It is not unusual to have a room full of weeping, writing adults who are recording long-forgotten moments.

FIVE SENSES

Most written descriptions center on sight and sound details, the dominant senses. This five-senses prewriting technique forces students to think about all of the senses involved and write a more alive narrative. Write columns for the five senses across the board:

Sight   **Sound**   **Taste**   **Smell**   **Touch**

Today we are going to discuss what it would be like to be one of the Egyptian workers in the handout picture. I want you to describe the scene in terms of the five senses. Let's begin by describing what you would see if you were one of these workers.

Record summary words in the columns as students talk. Examples you might give include "chiseling" or "breathing" in the sound column and "saliva" or "salt" in the taste column—just enough words to jar students' memories without giving them the writing details.

Then ask students to make their own columns of sensory details, borrowing any on the board that they like and adding to them with their own ideas. Give students five minutes to make a list. Then begin the writing assignment.

Independent Practice

1. Plan so that the writing is at least started, and preferably completed, immediately following the chosen prewriting activity. This is to ensure that ideas are fresh in students' minds and flowing. You might say,

   > 66 *You are now going to write a story in which you are the Egyptian worker helping to build a pyramid. This is called a first-person narrative. What pronoun will you use—I or he? Write quickly. Play the picture in your mind, like a movie scene, and then describe it with lots of details so that I can imagine the same scene.* 99

2. Put on very soft instrumental music in the classroom to ease the flow of writing. No talking allowed. Observe students writing without disrupting their concentration.

3. If it is obvious that a student is still stuck, just staring at the blank piece of paper, quietly engage the student in a direct-talking prewriting activity. Ask the student questions about the assignment that require details for answers. Then point to the empty page and say, "Write exactly what you just said to me." After one or a few times repeating this approach, the student can jump-start on his or her own.

4. All in-class writing assignments should be given a time limit—even if you later decide to give an extension. Time limits help procrastinators get moving. Also, sharing at the end—students voluntarily reading their writing to the class—is a great motivator for some students.

5. Give students class time to edit their writing for sentence errors. Emphasize "creativity first, mechanics last," but always insist that students clean up their writing before a formal presentation, such as turning it in to you.

Closure

Close by reminding students of what they learned and how they were successful:

> 66 *You have become familiar with a variety of prewriting, idea-gathering techniques that you will be able to use in the future. You were able to compose quickly when the writing step began, and you used specific details in your writing. With this assignment, as in all writing, you applied our class motto 'creativity first, mechanics last' and completed the final steps of editing and polishing.* 99

Evaluation

Use the Writing Rubric (page 165) for student self-evaluation and for your evaluation.

Reflection

- Ask students to share examples of how they reached the goals of this lesson. This could be an oral discussion or a writing assignment.

- Discuss with your students any aspects of flow that they experienced and add the information to the class flow chart (see page 5). Then ask students to make entries in their flow journals (see page 7).

Extension

- Encourage students to use prewriting techniques before any writing assignment, including to warm up and practice before an essay test.

- Have students develop and share their own prewriting techniques and tips.

Writing Rubric

Name:_____ Date:_____

	0	1	2	Points
Knowledge of subject matter	Writing does not show knowledge gained in history lesson	Writing includes a few facts from period	Writing reflects excellent command of facts from period	
Creativity	General writing only, doesn't say much	Writing includes a few specific details	Writing filled with concrete, sensory details	
On task in class	Student distracted class members from assigned work	Student was distracted during prewriting and writing activity	Student participated fully in the assigned work	
Sentence accuracy (if editing time allowed)	Many sentence errors	Some sentence errors	Few or no sentence errors	
			Total Points:	

Scoring:

8 = Excellent

7 = Very good

6 = Good

4–5 = Average

3 and below = Needs improvement

Chapter 19

Student-Created Math Games

Active Learning in Elementary Math

— Gina Lewis —

Student-Created Math Games

Math is a subject too easily ignored when it comes to enrichment activities. The following assignment requires students to create unique math games using the math skills they have developed up to this point. The instructions that follow are at a third-grade level; however, this lesson is easily modified to fit any grade level. Students are quite proud of their creations and eager to share them with their classmates. Working in groups could be an option for this assignment.

Materials

- ☐ Math Games Assignment Directions Page (page 170) for each student

- ☐ various materials for students to use to improvise games: bottles, cartons, caps, egg crates, boxes, tubes, cardboard from shirt inserts or cereal boxes, various containers, paper plates, and so on.

- ☐ student flow journals (see page 7)

Preparation

Collect materials in advance in case the students require them.

 ## Getting Students Excited about the Topic

1. Describe the project as a fun break from regular work:

   ❝ *Instead of working in your math book today, we are going to discuss a math project. In this project, you will create a math game of your very own!* ❞

2. Share the aims of the lesson so that students can relate to what they will achieve while having fun creating a game.

3. Explain that the game should use skills they have learned in math so far, and that they can use pieces from an existing game (such as dice or a gameboard) but the game has to be created by the student and cannot be an existing math game or other game.

4. Tell students that they will also need to write a directions sheet for playing the game. Hand out the Math Games Assignment Directions Page (page 170).

Guided Practice

Provide an example to get students started, such as the following:

❝ *I will show you an example of a math game that my daughter created when she was your age. We use a deck of cards and two players. Each player draws three cards and creates a multiplication problem, like 25 x 6 using the cards 2, 5, and 6. The other player does the same thing with his or her three cards. Whichever player creates the highest answer wins all the cards from that round. The game is over when one person has won all the cards. This game can be modified to fit almost any math problems, and you may have lowest answer win if you wish. Keep your minds open to using dice, gameboards, cards and other items. Be creative and have fun.* **❞**

Independent Practice

Students create their math games individually at home or in small groups. It is often better to have them do this at home because there simply is not enough material in one classroom for all the students to create their own games. Encourage them to try their games out before they bring them to the classroom because part of their grade is for the game to work without any glitches.

Closure

- Each student's game will be played in the classroom.
- Students will present short oral descriptions of their games and why they decided to make them the way they did.

Evaluation

Evaluate student creations according to the following criteria or your own criteria: turned in on time; directions sheet completed; playable game; effort; and creativity.

MY MATH GAME

Reflection

- Ask students to share examples of how they reached the goals of this lesson. This could be an oral discussion or a writing assignment.

- Discuss with your students any aspects of flow that they experienced and add the information to the class flow chart (see page 5). Then ask students to make entries in their flow journals (see page 7).

Extension

Create math game centers or a booth at the school carnival where people buy tickets to be contestants with the math game creators at their unique games; play during indoor recess; or share with another class by inviting the students to your room to play math games.

Math Games Assignment Directions Page

Due: _____

Project goal: To create a math game that uses math skills learned so far this year.

Your project should contain the following on your **typed** directions sheet:

☐ Game objective: what the player is trying to accomplish and learn.

☐ Number of players needed to play the game.

☐ List of the materials needed to play the game. For example: dice, gameboard, game pieces, cards, timers, buzzers, paper and pencil, and so on.

☐ Simple rules of the game. Remember, you don't want to confuse the players.

Keep in mind, your **typed** directions sheet should be clear enough for anyone to read and play your game without any questions. It would be a good idea to have someone else play your game before turning in the final product. Directions that might be easy for you to read could be confusing to someone else. Be creative and have fun!

Active Learning: Increasing Flow in the Classroom, © 2006 Crown House Publishing Company Ltd. • www.crownhouse.co.uk

Chapter 20

Guess-and-Check Tables

Active Learning to Solve Word Problems

— Marilyn Howard —

Grades: 5–8

Time Frame Options

30 to 40 minutes daily for five days (including evaluation on day 5)

Measurable Learning Objectives

Share these aims with students:

- *Students will follow and record the steps of a guess-and-check table model.*
- *Students will be able to check guesses from an organized table to establish a pattern.*
- *Students will use guess-and-check tables to determine solutions to a problem.*
- *Students will set the stage for writing equations to solve word problems.*

Guess-and-Check Tables

When students first begin to solve advanced word problems, they need to have a method to follow. The guess-and-check method enables students to solve problems easily before they are adept at converting word problems to algebraic equations. It lends itself well to solving problems algebraically later. The gamelike format of the guess-and-check model helps to keep students actively involved.

Materials

- ☐ standard math materials: students' math notebooks, pencils, and rulers
- ☐ highlighting pen for each student
- ☐ copy of the Solving Problems with Guess-and-Check Tables handout (page 178) for each student
- ☐ overhead projector and one transparency
- ☐ two colors of transparency pens
- ☐ student flow journals (see page 7)

Preparation

1. Review the lesson first to familiarize yourself with the method.

2. Photocopy the handout on page 178 for each student.

3. Write the basic problem on the board for students to see (or create a handout):

   "Sue and Ed are weighing their calves at the county fair. Ed's calf weighs 26 pounds less than Sue's. Together the calves weigh 212 pounds. How much does Sue's calf weigh?"

MATH IDEAS

 Getting Students Excited about the Topic

1. Share the objectives of the lesson so that students understand what they will accomplish. Explain that they will be learning a guessing strategy to solve word problems that will help them with future math problems, particularly algebra. For example:

> 66 *Today we will begin to use guess-and-check tables for solving word problems. Sometimes the easiest way to get started on a math problem is to guess what the answer might be and then check to see if you are right. Guessing is a good strategy for learning more about the problem, and it will lead to algebraic solutions later in the course.* 99

2. Connect the idea to past guessing students might have done in math and emphasize the importance of staying organized and neat while using the guess-and-check method:

> 66 *In the past, you have guessed at the answer to a problem and then figured out if you were right or wrong. A method called guess-and-check is a first step to mastering the power of algebra and solving problems. The problems you do in class should be well organized and readable. The organization is important. Your work should be neat and clear, like the examples you will see in class.* 99

Guided Practice

1. Explain the first problem to students and tell them that they are to try to help Sue and Ed figure out how much Sue's calf weighs by guessing based on what they do know.

> **"**Sometimes the easiest way to get started on a word problem is to guess a possible answer and then check to see how close you are. We will systematically arrive at our answer by organizing our guesses.**"**

2. Demonstrate the following steps on the overhead and have students write them down in their notebooks. Explain each step as you go.

Step 1: **"**Read the problem again. Sometimes it is helpful to sketch a picture, such as a drawing of two calves with a big "212" beneath them and a "26" between them. Use your ruler to set up a table. Decide what question is asked and summarize the question in the upper lefthand corner of your tables.**"**

Guess the weight of Sue's calf	

Step 2: **"**Make a guess and place this guess in the first column, beneath your summary of the problem. Leave plenty of room for other columns to the right of this first column. We will build our table one step at a time.
For our example, let's try guessing 130 pounds. Mark over the 130 with your highlighting pen to show that 130 is a guess.**"**

Guess the weight of Sue's calf	
130	

Step 3: **"**Assuming Sue's calf weighs 130 pounds, calculate how much Ed's calf weighs, knowing that Ed's calf weighs 26 pounds less than Sue's. Then label the heading for the second column. Be sure to highlight your guess of 130 every time you write it.**"**

Guess the weight of Sue's calf	Weight of Ed's calf
130	(130) – 26 = 104

Step 4: "*Now that you have possible weights for both Sue's and Ed's calves, you can calculate the total weight and label the third column "Total weight of both calves." Don't forget to highlight 130 when you write it again.*"

Guess the weight of Sue's calf	Weight of Ed's calf	Total weight of both calves
130	(130) – 26 = 104	(130) + 104 = 234

Step 5: "*Label the last column 'Check 212.' If your calculations of total weight did not equal 212 pounds, write in the last column whether the amount is 'too high' or 'too low.' If your total is 212 pounds, write 'correct.'*"

Guess the weight of Sue's calf	Weight of Ed's calf	Total weight of both calves	Check 212
130	(130) – 26 = 104	(130) + 104 = 234	too high

Step 6: "*If your total is too high or too low, start over with a new guess and use the same columns. Since the last guess was too high, Sue's calf must weigh less than 130 pounds. Try guessing 125 pounds and complete the second row of the table. Don't forget to highlight your guess.*"

Guess the weight of Sue's calf	Weight of Ed's calf	Total weight of both calves	Check 212
130	(130) – 26 = 104	(130) + 104 = 234	too high
125	(125) – 26 = 99	(125) + 99 = 224	too high

Step 7: "*Our answer is getting closer, but it is still too high. Try 115 pounds. Complete the third row.*"

Guess the weight of Sue's calf	Weight of Ed's calf	Total weight of both calves	Check 212
130	(130) – 26 = 104	(130) + 104 = 234	too high
125	(125) – 26 = 99	(125) + 99 = 224	too high
115	(115) – 26 = 89	(115) + 89 = 204	too low

Step 8: ❝*Our guess of 115 pounds is too low, but now we know that the answer is between 125 pounds and 115 pounds, and that 115 pounds is a little bit closer. Try 119 pounds.*❞

Guess the weight of Sue's calf	Weight of Ed's calf	Total weight of both calves	Check 212
130	(130) – 26 = 104	(130) + 104 = 234	too high
125	(125) – 26 = 99	(125) + 99 = 224	too high
115	(115) – 26 = 89	(115) + 89 = 204	too low
119	(119) – 26 = 93	(119) + 93 = 212	correct

Step 9: ❝*Congratulations! You have found the correct answer. Now you have only one thing left to do. Write a complete sentence that answers the question asked in the problem: Sue's calf weighs 119 pounds.*❞

Independent Practice

1. Students could work on these problems individually, in groups, or as a whole class. Explain the first problem to students and have them write it down.

   ❝*I am thinking of a number. If you add 5 to the number and then multiply the sum by 7, you get 91. What is my number?*❞

2. Ask if anyone needs to have the problem repeated to make sure everyone gets the details down.

3. Demonstrate the column headings for the guess-and-check table on the overhead for students to copy and use to solve the problem (the answer is 8).

Guess the number	Add 5 to the number	Multiply sum by 7	Check 91

4. Remind students to write their answers as complete sentences.

5. Try a second problem. For example:

   ❝*I am thinking of a number. First, multiply it by 6, and then subtract 7. The result is 83. What is my number?*❞

6. This time, have students create their own tables. The headings should be similar to this:

Guess number	Multiply by 6	Subtract 7	Check 83

7. Walk around to check student work. (The correct guess in this case will be 15.)

Closure

Hand out Solving Problems with Guess-and-Check Tables (page 178) for students to keep for future reference, or have them write down the steps of the guess-and-check method in their notebooks.

Evaluation

- The first evaluation should be in pairs. Photocopy the pairs quiz on page 179 for each pair or re-create it for students. (The quiz answers are Cinder = 6, Rusty = 12, Gary = 9.)

- After students are comfortable with the procedure, evaluate them individually. Photocopy the individual quiz on page 180 for each student or re-create it. (The quiz answers are Matt = 54, Zach = 86.)

- Use the Guess-and-Check Rubric for grading the process, as well as grading correct answers.

Reflection

- Discuss with your students any aspects of flow they experienced and add the information to the class flow chart (see page 5). Ask students to make entries in their flow journals (see page 7).

- Ask students to share examples of how they reached the goals of this lesson. This could be an oral discussion or a writing assignment.

Extension

Students could create word problems for each other to solve using guess-and-check tables. Each student would also create a guess-and-check answer key for each word problem.

Solving Problems with Guess-and-Check Tables

1. Read the problem carefully. Make notes or sketch a picture to organize the information in the problem.

2. Look at the question asked in the problem and set up a table with that question in the first column. Leave extra space for more columns in case you need them.

3. Decide what you are going to guess.

4. Create a new column to calculate the problem using your guess. Create as many columns as you need for each step of the calculation.

5. Create a last column for checking your guess. Write in "too low," "too high," or "correct" for each guess.

6. Calculate the table until the check is correct.

7. Write the answer in a complete sentence.

Example: The sum of two consecutive numbers is 37. What are the numbers?

Guess first number	Second number (hint: the second consecutive number is always one more than the first)	Total of numbers (sum)	Check 37
10	(10) + 1 = 11	(10) + 11 = 21	too low
20	(20) + 1 = 21	(20) + 21 = 41	too high
17	(17) + 1 = 18	(17) + 18 = 35	too low
18	(18) + 1 = 19	(18) + 19 = 37	correct

The sum of the two consecutive numbers 18 and 19 is 37.

Active Learning: Increasing Flow in the Classroom, © 2006 Crown House Publishing Company Ltd. • www.crownhouse.co.uk

Guess-and-Check Pairs Quiz

Fill out a guess-and-check table for the following problem. Don't forget to write your answer in a sentence.

Miss Howe has three cats. The youngest cat is Cinder. Rusty is twice as old as Cinder, and Gary is 3 years older than Cinder. Together their ages total 27 years. How old is Cinder? More columns may be necessary.

Guess Cinder's age		

Guess-and-Check Individual Quiz

Fill out a guess-and-check table for the following problem. Don't forget to write your answer in a sentence.

Matt and Zach were selling giftwrap orders. Zach sold 32 orders more than Matt did. All together, they sold 140 orders. How many did each one sell?

Guess # of orders Matt sold	# of orders Zach sold (Matt + 32)	Total orders sold	Check 140

Guess-and-Check Rubric

Name:_____ Date:_____

	0	**1**	**2**	**3**	**Points**
Understanding of guess-and-check tables	Shows little or no grasp of how to use guess-and-check tables	Shows limited grasp of using guess-and-check tables	Shows essential grasp of using guess-and-check tables	Shows full grasp and use of guess-and-check tables	
Recorded completion of steps and sentence	Recorded work is barely (if at all) comprehensible	Recorded work is incomplete, somewhat misdirected, or not clearly presented	Recorded one or two steps, but answer not in a complete sentence	Recorded all necessary steps and used a complete sentence for the answer	
				Total Points:	

Scoring:

6 = Fully accomplished purpose of task

4–5 = Substantially accomplished purpose of task

2–3 = Partly accomplished purpose of task

0–1 = Made little or no progress toward accomplishing task

Chapter 21

Animal Studies in 18 Steps

Active Learning in Science

— Gina Lewis —

Animal Studies in 18 Steps

This unit helps students understand that all of life and learning are connected. Teachers want students to realize their potential and their belonging in a world where learning never ends. The goal is for them to think independently with motivation and curiosity.

Students need to become active in their own learning, and this only happens when we give them some control over the direction of their learning. This chapter provides a format for independent study that can be easily modified for a wide range of grade levels. In this independent research unit, students choose a topic to study, employ all disciplines, practice time-management skills, create products, and experience mastery by teaching others about what they learned through research.

Materials

- ☐ Animal Studies Directions Page (page 187) for each student
- ☐ Animal Studies Progress Checklist (page 188) for each student
- ☐ folders for student work
- ☐ world map
- ☐ student flow journals (see page 7)
- ☐ various research materials

Preparation

1. Photocopy the directions page and checklist for students.

2. Read through the chapter to get a sense of the research materials you might have available for students, such as encyclopedias, nonfiction books on animals, library time, Internet access (and perhaps specific sites marked for students), children's periodicals about animals and nature, and so forth.

3. Set dates for when you will review student progress on their checklists, when students should complete the unit, and when students will teach the class about their animals.

Grades: 1–8

Time Frame Options

30 to 40 minutes a day for a total of 21 days

Measurable Learning Objectives

Share these aims with students:

- Students will each create a notebook containing their research.
- Students will each create a product of their choice that relies on their research (such as a poster, diorama, puppet, and so on).
- Students will teach the class using the research and projects they have accumulated through this unit.
- Students will learn valuable time-management skills by having to pace their work to meet deadlines.

Getting Students Excited about the Topic

1. Introduce the unit as a chance for students to research their favorite animals and become experts on them. Explain the aims of the lesson so that students understand and can relate to the learning objectives. Be sure to give them a sense of the benefits of the study to motivate them. For example:

   “ *Think of an animal that you would like to know more about, or think about an animal that has always been your favorite. Some of my favorite animals are very unusual, like the sloth or the lemur. How would you like to spend the year becoming an expert on this particular animal? Once you have completed this study, you will experience mastery and be the expert in the classroom about your animal.* **”**

2. Explain that students will pursue an area of study each day to learn more about their animals. They will keep the day's work in a folder, which they will use later in products and to teach the class about their animals.

Guided Practice

During the first three days of the unit, students choose an animal and learn more from you about what they will be doing.

Day 1: Students choose an animal and read about it.

Day 2: Students write about what they know and what they would like to know about their animal, and then share their answers with the class.

Day 3: Review and discuss the Animal Studies Directions Page (page 187) and the progress checklist (page 188). Have each student fill in the name of the animal in the blanks of the directions page to personalize it. (Remember that each step may be easily modified to fit your program.) The special interest project (step 16) is a project that students will present during the "teach the class" time (step 18). Teaching the class should be done at the very end so that the students have completed their research before teaching about the animal.

Independent Practice

1. Now the fun begins! Students complete the 18 steps on the directions page in any order they wish, except for steps 17 and 18, which must come last.

2. Students keep track of their progress on the checklist. When they finish a step, they write the date beside the step on the checklist and ask a classmate to double-check their work and initial the checklist, next to the step and date. Decide when you will check student progress and let students know the dates. Also set a date for completion of the unit.

3. Before students get started, remind them once more of the point of the research:

   66 *Remember, you are researching your animal to become a master of this subject.* **99**

Closure

Once the students have taught the class, restate and reinforce that they have achieved mastery through their research on that animal.

Evaluation

- Evaluate the special interest projects based on quantity and quality of information, neatness and organization, and how well students followed directions.

- Evaluate how well each student teaches the class based on the following criteria: knowledge about the animal, use of appropriate materials, clear speaking voice, interesting teaching, organization, and preparation.

- The students will assess one another's progress through the unit every week.

Reflection

- Ask students to share examples of how they reached the goals of this lesson. This could be an oral discussion or a writing assignment.

■ Discuss with your students any aspects of flow that they experienced and add the information to the class flow chart (see page 5). Then ask students to make entries in their flow journals (see page 7).

Extension

■ This unit can be modified to fit any other area of study, such as mathematicians and their discoveries, communities, our nation, habitats, poetry and poets, myths and fables, or artists.

■ Any step in the unit could be expanded. For example, students could perform music and recitations for others beyond the class (such as for other classes or parents), play student games at recess or in physical education class, create a word wall using the vocabulary words, display reports and projects, perform a play, go on field trips, create bulletin boards and information centers, and post the newsletters online.

■ Arrange with zoo docents or Animal Sanctuary employees to have animal visitors come to school.

Animal Studies Directions Page

Fill all the blanks with the name of the animal you chose to study. Then complete each step for that animal.

1. **Science**—List 10 scientific facts about _____.
2. **Geography**—List 10 facts about _____'s habitat and pinpoint the environment on the world map.
3. **Math**—Create 10 factual story problems with answers based on what you know about _____.
4. **Reading**—Create a bibliography of resources for information about _____ and give a book report about one of the resources.
5. **Writing**—Write and illustrate a story or poem in which _____ is the main character, or create a newspaper front page story about _____.
6. **Spelling**—Make a spelling list of 10 words related to _____.
7. **History**—How has _____ affected humanity throughout history? Explain in one page.
8. **Music**—Create and perform any type of music related to _____. This can be a song, rap, cheer, or an instrumental piece. You may do it in front of the class or on videotape. You will present this when you teach the class.
9. **Journal**—How has _____ affected you? How do you feel about _____? Why?
10. **Art**—Make a picture, poster, collage, sculpture, or painting of _____ to present when you teach the class.
11. **Online newsletter**—Research and report 10 facts about _____ to add to the class newsletter.
12. **Recitation**—Create or find a quotation about _____ and recite it for the class during your presentation.
13. **Vocabulary**—Make a list of 10 words with definitions related to _____.
14. **Game**—Create a game for P.E. class or a board game about _____. Write the rules and the results of playing the game in your folder.
15. **Foreign language**—In a foreign language, write and speak five words about _____.
16. **Special interest project**—Meet with your teacher to create an assignment that you are especially interested in doing concerning _____. This will be graded and become part of your overall grade. Present it when you teach the class.
17. **KWL**—Complete the essay you began about what you know and would like to know about _____ by writing everything that you have learned about your animal.
18. **Teach the class**—Schedule this with your teacher and use at least five of the steps that you have worked on in your presentation. This will be graded and become part of your overall grade.

Animal Studies Progress Checklist

Under "date completed" write the date that you completed each step on the Animal Studies Directions Page. Ask a classmate to double-check your work for you and initial the "checked by" column.
I will periodically ask that this checklist be turned in.

Animal study step	Date completed	Checked by
1. Science		
2. Geography		
3. Math		
4. Reading		
5. Writing		
6. Spelling		
7. History		
8. Music		
9. Journal		
10. Art		
11. Newsletter		
12. Recitation		
13. Vocabulary		
14. Game		
15. Foreign language		
16. Special interest project		
17. KWL		
18. Teach the class		

References

Castro, J. 1985. *The Art and Life of Georgia O'Keeffe.* New York: Crown Publishers.

Chambers, J. 2003. *Ready, Set, Read: Building a Love of Letters and Literacy through Fun Phonics Activities.* Tucson, Ariz.: Zephyr Press.

Clark, K. 1969. *Civilization.* New York: Harper and Row.

Cole, B., and A. Gealt. 1989. *Art of the Western World.* New York: Summit Books.

Copland, A. 2003. *Copland Conducts Copland.* New York: Sony Music Entertainment [CD].

Covey, S. 1989. *The Seven Habits of Highly Effective People.* New York: Simon and Schuster.

Csikszentmihalyi, M. 1990. *Flow: The Psychology of Optimal Experience.* New York: Harper and Row.

———. 1996. *Creativity: Flow and the Psychology of Discovery and Invention.* New York: Harper Collins.

———. 1997. *Finding Flow: The Psychology of Engagement with Everyday Life.* New York: Basic Books.

Dalgiesh, A. 2000. *The Courage of Sarah Noble.* New York: Simon and Schuster.

Forbes, E. 1969. *Johnny Tremain.* New York: Dell.

Forty, S. 1998. *The World of Art.* London: PRC Publishing.

Griffin, J. B. 1977. *Phoebe the Spy.* New York: Scholastic.

Grun, B. 1991. *The Timetables of History.* New York: Simon and Schuster/Touchstone.

Herman, G., and P. Hollingsworth. 2001. *Kinetic Kaleidoscope.* Tulsa, Okla.: University School at the University of Tulsa.

Hollingsworth, P., ed. 2000. *Student Active Interdisciplinary Learning Series Curriculum Kit.* Tulsa, Okla.: University School at the University of Tulsa. (Available online at www.uschool.utulsa.edu and www.clickandlearn.com.)

Jensen, E. 2001. *Arts with the Brain in Mind.* Alexandria, Va.: ASCD.

Jerome-Cohen, D. 1994. *Literature and Writing Workshop: Exploring Plays.* New York: Scholastic.

Korty, C. 1986. *Writing Your Own Plays: Creating, Adapting, Improvising.* New York: Macmillan.

Margulies, N., and C. Valenza. 2005. *Visual Thinking: Tools for Mapping Your Ideas.* Norwalk, Conn.: Crown House Publishing.

McGovern, A. 1975. *The Secret Soldier.* New York: Scholastic.

Munro, R., and D. Maddex. 1986. *Architects Make Zigzags.* Washington, D.C.: Preservation Press.

Murray, P. 1978. *Renaissance Architecture.* New York: Abram.

Neret, G. 2004. *Rubens.* Hohensollernring, Germany: Taschen.

Nunhead, N. 1994. *Claude Monet.* Greenwich, Conn.: Brompton Books.

Olson, J. 1992. *Envisioning Writing: Toward an Integration of Drawing and Writing.* Portsmouth, N.H.: Heinemann Educational Books.

Rea, D. 2003. "Optimal Motivation for Creative Intelligence." In *Creative Intelligence: Toward Theoretic Integration,* ed. D. Ambrose, L. M. Cohen, and A. Tannenbaum, 211-35. Cresskill, N.J.: Hampton Press.

Restak, R. 2001. *Mozart's Brain and the Fighter Pilot: Unleashing Your Brain's Potential.* New York: Three Rivers Press.

Rose, L. 2001. *Easy Reading: Finding Joy and Meaning in Words.* Tucson, Ariz.: Zephyr Press.

Scherer, M. 2002. "Do Students Care About Learning? A Conversation with Mihaly Csikszentmihalyi." *Educational Leadership* 60 (1): 12–17.

Shanor, K. 1999. *The Emerging Mind.* Los Angeles: Renaissance Books.

Smith, A. 2005. *Move It: Physical Movement and Learning.* Norwalk, Conn.: Crown House Publishing.

Sylwester, R. 1995. *A Celebration of Neurons.* Alexandria, Va.: ASCD.

——. 2004. "The Deep Roots of the Arts." Connecting Brain Processes to School Policies and Practices (July). *Brain Connection,* www.brainconnection.com/content/205_1 (accessed August 5, 2005).

Toman, R. ed. 1998. *Baroque: Architecture, Sculpture, Painting.* Cologne, Germany: Könemann.

Weber, J. A. 2000. *Architecture Everywhere: Investigating the Built Environment of Your Community.* Tucson, Ariz.: Zephyr Press.

White, E. B. 1980. *Charlotte's Web.* New York: Scholastic.

Whiting, R. 1998. *Leonardo: A Portrait of a Renaissance Man.* New York: Knickerbocker Press.

Wilson, F. 1988. *What It Feels Like to Be a Building.* Washington, D.C.: Preservation Press.

Wolfe, P. 2001. *Brain Matters: Translating Research into Classroom Practice.* Alexandria, Va.: ASCD.

Wooden, J. 2003. *Inch and Miles: The Journey to Success.* Logan, Iowa: Perfection Learning.

Wooden, J., and S. Jamison. 1997. *Wooden: A Lifetime of Observations and Reflections On and Off the Court.* Lincolnwood, Ill.: Contemporary Books.

Authors and Contributors

Pat Hollingsworth is the director of University School at the University of Tulsa in Oklahoma. In addition to her duties as director, she teaches art, kindergarten, and university graduate classes. She is a board member of the National Association for Gifted Children; coauthor of *Smart Art* and *Kinetic Kaleidoscope;* and editor, illustrator, and coauthor of the SAILS (Students Active Interdisciplinary Learning Series) Curriculum Kit, an interdisciplinary humanities course for students of all ages. (SAILS is available at www.uschool.utulsa. edu/ and through www.clickandlearn.com.) Pat has given presentations on her books and articles in Canada, Mexico, Europe, and widely in the United States.

Gina Lewis is the third-grade teacher at University School at the University of Tulsa in Oklahoma. She is a board member of the Oklahoma Association for Gifted and Creative Teachers, a U.S. Department of Education Javits grant teacher, and a coauthor of the SAILS Curriculum Kit. She is trained in the use of Kumon math, IIM, and Great Expectations and has given presentations on gifted education at state and national levels. She was a nominee twice for Disney's outstanding teacher award. She is currently completing her master's degree in gifted education at the University of Tulsa. Most recently, she won a Fund for Teachers educational grant to travel and study in Italy.

Contributors

Katie Abercrombie teaches middle school language arts at University School at the University of Tulsa. She has a B.A. in journalism, has a master's in business administration, and is a member of Phi Beta Kappa. She was formerly a Tulsa newspaper reporter and a composition instructor at the local community college. She was a U.S. Department of Education Javits grant teacher for six summers. Katie is a coauthor of the SAILS Curriculum Kit and has been nominated for Who's Who in American Education.

Marilyn Cox teaches fifth- and sixth-grade social studies and language arts at University School at the University of Tulsa. She is a coauthor of the SAILS Curriculum Kit and was a U.S. Department of Education Javits grant teacher. She has presented at state and national gifted education conferences. Marilyn received her master's in gifted education from the University of Tulsa; raising her own gifted children provided invaluable experience.

Donna Davilla, MFA, was the gifted and talented and art consultant for the Des Moines Public Schools in Des Moines, Iowa. She studied the Reggio Emilia early childhood program in Reggio Emilia, Italy, and the multiple intelligences with Howard Gardner, through Project Zero at Harvard University. Both programs emphasize the arts as a means to disseminate the curriculum. She co-authored an article for the *NAEA Journal* about adapting the Reggio approach to public education. Donna has presented nationally at art, gifted and talented, and magnet school education conferences. She was a delegate on an Art Education Federation to the Middle East trip and has been an FL Wright fellow at Fallingwater, Bear Run, Pennsylvania. She is presently an independent art consultant and can be contacted at ddavilla1@earthlink.net.

Arlene DeVries is the community resource consultant for the gifted and talented program in Des Moines, Iowa. She has taught music to K–12 and has used "Copland's Rodeo" with all ages, including her adult education class called "Learning to Enjoy Classical Music." For more than 15 years, she has presented the lecture one hour prior to each Des Moines Symphony concert. She is president of SENG (Supporting Emotional Needs of the Gifted) and a member of the board of the National Association for Gifted Children. With Dr. James T. Webb, she coauthored the book *Gifted Parent Groups: The SENG Model*. She received the Iowa Talented and Gifted Association's Distinguished Service Award in 2003.

Stacy Hale has taught high school English at Washington High School in Washington, Oklahoma, for the past ten years. She attends Enclyomedia and AP conventions in the state. She has begun work on her master's at Oklahoma University.

Gail N. Herman, Ph.D., is an educational arts consultant and a professional storyteller. She teaches education, enrichment, and arts-related courses for Garrett College, Lesley University, and the University of Connecticut's Confrat-ute. Gail serves on several boards, including the Association for the Education of Gifted Underachieving Students and the YOUTH Special Interest Group of the National Storytelling Network. She is a contributing editor for *Roeper Review*.

Marilyn Howard is the seventh- and eighth-grade math and computer teacher at University School at the University of Tulsa. In addition to teaching, she has been a MATHCOUNTS coach for 12 years and an Academic Bowl coach for 9 years. She was the Mathematical Association of America's Outstanding Math Teacher for Oklahoma in the year 2000. She has made math presentations at both the state and the national levels for gifted education and at the national level for the National Council of Teachers of Mathematics. She is a coauthor of the SAILS Curriculum Kit and was a U.S. Department of Education Javitz grant teacher.

Elizabeth Jarnigan has a master's degree in physical education from Fort Hays State in Hays, Kansas. She taught physical education at Carleton College in Northfield, Minnesota, for three years. She also taught at Burnsville High School in Burnsville, Minnesota; Bethel College in North Newton, Kansas; and Briar Cliff College in Sioux City, Iowa. Liz is currently the life skills coordinator for academics and compliance in athletics at the University of Tulsa.

Alicia Parent is a teacher at University School at the University of Tulsa. She has a master's degree in gifted education and has presented at numerous conferences for both the Oklahoma Association for Gifted, Creative, and Talented and the National Association for Gifted and Talented. She is a coauthor of the SAILS Curriculum Kit and was a U.S. Department of Education Javits grant teacher for six years.

Index